His Priceless Pearls Unfolding

The Pearl of Great Price

E. C.

WestBow
PRESS

A DIVISION of THOMAS NELSON

WestBow Press books may be ordered through booksellers or by contacting:

WestBow Press
A Division of Thomas Nelson
1663 Liberty Drive
Bloomington, IN 47403
www.westbowpress.com
1-(866) 928-1240

I used KJV of Bible exclusively- except where indicated,
also I used Merriam- Webster Dictionary

Front cover art drawn by—E. C.

ISBN: 978-1-4497-7647-3 (sc)

Library of Congress Control Number: 2012921928

Printed in the United States of America

WestBow Press rev. date: 01/17/2013

"...Fame and fortune are fleeting, but His flame last forever..."

[Notation: as far as I know this quote was given to me, by the Holy Spirit]

~

"Then shall that wicked be revealed, with the spirit of his mouth, and shall destroy with the brightness of his second coming...2Ths. 2:8"

~

"Foxes have holes, and the birds of the air have nest; but the son of man has nowhere to rest his head...beloved you are now my resting place and I am your Sabbath."

~

"Let us be glad and rejoice and give honor to him: for the marriage of the Lamb is come and his bride makes herself ready...Rev. 19: 7"

~

"Love as brilliant as the Son consumes the bride and destroys the Enemy"

~

Shekinah is a word that is not used in scripture, but it is significant, It comes from the Hebrew root, sk-k-n, meaning to dwell *Shekinah is used by the Rabbis to speak of the presences of God,* which is 'automatically accompanied by, <u>brilliant light</u> so <u>*His presence*</u> is associated with <u>*Shekinah*</u>. Called the <u>*divine presence,*</u> *Shekinah as a feminine noun speaks of God's feminine attributes of mercy and love.* A related word is *mishkin,* meaning tabernacle, most often used for the tabernacle of Moses, but sometimes translated *"DWELLING PLACE"* and very few times referring to David's tabernacle. Reference the "POWER THE NEW TESTMENT" glossary, pg. 405

Evelyn Colarelli

Dedication

My first desire is 'to humbly thank Father, Son, and Holy Spirit for my salvation and the gifts and callings on my life. For without the gifts I would not have had the privilege to writing this book. Now, I am able to share it with those who will read it. To thank all my children and grandchildren who will never know the "heavy price" we all paid so that I would come to a place where God could use me, until the day they stand before the Lord. Thank you Lord Jesus for turning what the enemy meant for evil in to good for me and mine, they do not see it now but they will one day. To my precious granddaughter I 'thank you Keeley, for your love, and encouragement (to wright this book) through the years for I believe you were the extra grace I "was given to keep me going. I also want to thank you Georgia P. for your friendship, prayers, and encouragement.

Epigraph

Hear, Oh Israel, this is my beloved and this is my friend, oh daughters of Jerusalem, for when we fall in love with Jesus, nothing matters but him!

Beloved church we must walk in the Holy Spirit of God's love, for the wisdom of God's love is forgiveness.

When born of God we learn to walk in our Lord Loves embrace, the world fades, and our giving to the kingdom of God, in his name, in secret (*prayer*) 'is magnified. Then with purified hearts, we will honor him with our gifts and callings like this: a penny (prayer) given with a humble heart does more to further the kingdom of God than a million dollars from a pride-filled heart. For beloved, we cannot buy our way into Gods' good graces, favor, and blessings, for he has freely given to us "all things." For God sent his only begotten Son into the world that we might live through him...walking as he did sowing seeds of his love not sowing seeds of money...as we give in secret he will reward us openly.

Believe me when I say, from experience, when I fell in Love with Jesus all that I had, "has become his" family, home, money my habitual sinful nature everything! As I learned to obey the word, nothing did I withhold from him for his beauty is always before me. By the Holy Spirits leading and guiding teaching me to "hear his voice and no other"! As I begun to walk up right before him, trusting knowing that as I let go of each of these things especially my children he would take eternal care of them walking by faith not sight as I continue to grow in him, no longer did I care what man thought of me for I just wanted to honor him.

Beloved we will see the beauty in adversity when we trust in the Lord.

I would like to share a happy little Ditty the Holy Spirit gave me, with you, it goes like this...Yedi he' Yedi hi' Yedi ho' ho' Christ is being formed in me and he will complete the good work he has begun in you and me!

E. C.

The Pearl of Great Price

The church/pearl is formed through much suffering (Matt. 13:45–46; Rev 1:18, 19:6–10).

As Jesus' bride is humbled under the mighty hand of God, she cries out, "I want to be more like you, Jesus! Because of God's great grace in her life, in her death throes she will cry out to herself with a loud voice, *"Eli, Eli, lama sabachthani!,"* which means, "My God, my God, why have you forsaken me!" In this way she too will have yielded up herself to the Holy Ghost, for Jesus' bride walks parallel to her Beloved and will suffer for the sake of the gospel, Christ's message (Matt. 27:46, 50; Phil. 3:10).

Dear Jewish and Gentile bride, come and take a spiritual journey with me through these pages in time, as the Holy Spirit has revealed to me who the true bride of Jesus Christ is! The Lord is so hauntingly beautiful; his beauty transcends space and time. Mere words alone cannot express the beauty of the Lord; you have to experience it. It changed me forever. He emptied my cup to fill me up with himself.

Contents

Introduction

This book 'will not read like any book you have ever read before, for it is a diary of the Lord's love for me, and my love for him. Be blessed and encouraged for we who love him 'will be transformed in the twinkling of an eye. Beloved, remember that where your heart is there your treasure will be also (Matt. 6:19–21).

Now is the time to come to the unity of the Holy Spirit. For the Spirit and the bride say, "Come!" The Lord is calling, shaking us to *wake up'* his Jewish and Gentile bride! She has been dormant and hidden from view, lying dormant for so long, becoming lethargic because of false doctrines (Song 2:1–17, Isa. 52:2–15; 60:1–22). Arise, beloved! Arise and shine!

I pray you will be blessed' and encouraged, by the contents of this book, for we all have our gifts and callings to further the kingdom of God and we desperately need one another and separated too long. We must put on the whole *armor* of God to become the whole *army* of God in order to defeat the enemy (1 Pet. 1:1).

After many years, I can finally see what the Lord is doing in my life and the wonderful changes he has made in my heart. He said he kept me on a short line, for he was training me on the battlefield of affliction! Then, on October 21, 2005, in the evening, he continued in this same vain. He said, "I have trained you in this way, for even I learned to obey through the things I suffered! Ultimately, you will come to a place where you will esteem others better than self-will. Willingly dying to your own will so that *my* will is done in you, you will further the kingdom of God in picking up your cross daily to follow me.

He continued, saying, "I trained you in this way so as not to withhold your free will, knowing that you would become submissive and yielding, thus surrendering to the Father's will for your life. His great love is his will for us, and it 'will be done on earth, in our earthen vessels, as it is in heaven. For the Father's body of believers is a many-membered body, and you will be trained, tried, tested, and found true, and then you will be placed within the body according to the Father's good will and pleasure, not for her glory but for the Father's glory.

My Lord went on to say to me, "You are no longer bull-headed, but I have made you bold and persistent in me and for me. Then he pointed out that he wanted me to look up the definitions of some words in the dictionary that I might better understand what he was saying to me and what he was doing. Here are the words and their meanings.

- *Forward*: (1) Being near or at or belonging to the front; (2) eager, ready; (3) brash, bold; (4) Notably advanced or developed, precocious; (5) Moving, tending, or leading toward a position in front.

- *Line*: the forward position in warfare where one must be bold, daring, fearless
- *Presumptuous*: to be bold or forward, about this word, the Lord said, "You must not be overly bold or forward for me; yet this is the way some people perceive you at times."
- *Persistent*: continuing, especially in the face of opposition, etc.; continuing to exist or endure constantly in spite of adversity.
- *Constant*: coming together, standing, not changing, faithful, regular, stable, etc.; continual; persistent in anything that does not change or vary
- *Affliction*: pain, suffering, any cause of suffering In this, he said that I follow Him blindly.
- *Blind*: without the power of sight; lacking insight; hard to see; not controlled by intelligence; to make sightless; to dazzle; a place of concealment; 'a decoy for a season.

I was crying and very humbled by the time I looked these words up and tried to understand them all. Then the Lord said, "I have put you in a position to take the fire. Nevertheless, this is just for a season, my beloved. I will bring you out of the heat of your battle wilderness! This has been for your preparation."

I said, "Gee, thanks, Lord," and in my spirit, I heard him laugh.

He said that he takes the weak to confound the strong (1 Cor. 1:27–28), and he always saves the best wine for last. I did, not continue to cry as I began to ponder his words to me, for I do not highly esteem myself, nor did I ever. I had very little understanding at this time and was very puzzled by his words. Then, as I began to understand, I rejoiced in these words, for I had begun to realize that I was standing with many others who 'had been crushed and made weak in order to become strong in and through God. Through the privilege of knowing him and the fellowship of his suffering, I understood that what I endure is nothing compared to what he endured for me!

For instance, as powerful as Paul (Saul) was, he was made weak and blind so he could see Jesus clearly, becoming weak in the flesh to become strong in the spirit. This was a place of total surrender for Paul. He 'was brought to his knees, made blind by the light of the Lord, becoming totally helpless and humbled in order for God to bless him and transform him from Saul into Paul. He 'was made sightless so he could see in the spirit in order to further God's kingdom.

Changing Saul's name to Paul, God used him to the "anti-degree," or total opposite, of who he had been (2 Cor. 5:7). No longer would Paul go by what he could see, hear, or feel; now in his weakness he would proclaim to the world, "Faith is the substance of things hoped for, the evidence of things not seen." Paul was truly humbled under the mighty hand of God.

Moreover, anyone that the Lord Jesus uses in this hour 'will be humbled by such a personal revelation. I said, "Let it be according to your word, my Lord. Your will be done in my life."

Beloved, we must choose to agree on those things where we can agree—on the Father, Son, and Holy Spirit of the living God—and stop focusing on those things we disagree. We are to forsake man's ways, pick up our crosses daily, and follow Jesus, for He is the only way. Hear what the Spirit is saying to the churches, for many of us 'are called, but too few agree to be chosen. He knows his own and they know him, for they hear his voice and follow him. God is saying, "Make up your mind. Quit your duplicity. Are you for me or against me?" Please, read the epistle of James in the King James Version of the Bible may the Holy Spirit open up, your understanding.

"Unite in my love," says the Lord, "or be crippled by your own self-righteousness!" We can accept or reject this. I choose to hear His voice and no other. This song is ringing in my ears: "Bind us together, Lord. Bind us together, Lord, with your love." We sang this song in the Catholic Church, and I love all those who love my Lord Jesus. For he is no respecter of persons his beloved is hidden in him. In every denomination, there are those who have accepted him and love him. I am trembling even now, for I have a reverential fear, a respect for the Lord and his beloved. We will give account for every idle word we have spoken against one another. Who are we that we can judge one another? This is nit-picking, self-righteous behavior!

We are to *try* the spirits to see if they are of God, not *judge* them. That is the Lord's work. I cry, "Abba, Father, help me to be willing, to be willing to do your will! My desire and prayer is to decrease so that you will increase in me: less of me, and more of you Lord! Then I too will proclaim as Paul did, 'It is not I who live but Christ.' Father, unless I decrease, I will be of no use to you and your kingdom. Help me, Holy Spirit!"

Do you not know that the enemy is uniting his "false church," for he counterfeits everything God is doing in the natural and in the spirit? The enemy is the author of confusion, not of peace and a sound mind. Around the time, I wrote this message, a minister spoke angry words over me. He said that I was a wheel without many spokes. These words confused me, until the Lord said, "That's okay, Evelyn. You have three spokes: the Father, Son, and Holy Spirit. You, my bride-church, are the fourth spoke, and she has many members, and my church always depends on the Trinity for her stability or she will be out of balance! The Trinity is a balancing force or influence counteracting the effect of the enemy."

I said, "Thank you, Lord, for clearing up my confusion."

"Earth, creation, and world: four proceeds from three and depends upon three (Gen. 2:10; Lev. 11:20–27; Mark 16:15).

With this revelation, I shouted, "Yes, Lord, yes! Glory hallelujah and amen!" Then I began to pray, "Father, humble us so we will unite in the Holy Spirit, please, for hurting people hurt each other. Bathe us; heal us from past hurts with the fire of your love!"

If we have spoken against one another, we must repent, for we are to bless and not curse. God loves us so much that he is not willing that any man should perish but that all should come to repentance. In forgiving one another, we will come into the full knowledge of his dear Son, our Lord Jesus Christ. Then the Lord began speaking about his mother Mary: her ministry was to birth him into the natural world. She 'was chosen because of her bloodline, not her sinless nature, for she was human, and her Son had not died for her sins yet.

He loved her so much! He was saying that his mother suffered greatly for the kingdom's sake—before and after his birth. The Lord says that we are to honor her and *all* mothers for their love and care of God's children. Our Lord says that Mary was very beautiful and humble—a type and shadow of her Son's virtuous bride, gracious within adversity, putting her faith in the Father and being submissive to the Holy Spirit. Now, my beloved, hear what the Holy Spirit is saying to the church.

The Lord's bride walks in the Spirit, not fulfilling the lust of the flesh, and in this she and the Holy Spirit will birth the children of God into his kingdom. For those led by the Spirit are the sons, children of God. Rom. 8:1–39 Jesus' second coming based on our readiness for him, having our oil lamps full, and only the Father knows the hour and day this will be. As we wait and yield to the Holy Spirit in preparation for our Lord, the Holy Spirit is cleansing and purifying us to be whole and holy, without spot or wrinkle before our Lord and King Jesus Christ. Eph. 5:25–27

The Lord speaks: "The cross was and is the only way I could set you free. Now it is your turn to pick up your cross and follow me, for the harvest is plenty but the laborers are few! For there is too few who would will die for my kingdom's sake! Some are too busy focusing on the things and cares of this world and they no longer hear me, for they have left their first love and drifted far from me—too far to hear my voice. Moreover, they refuse to repent! For their false pride and the things of this world 'has become their God Lucifer. So now, I have released them to the Enemy's destruction for their own sakes! With a heavy heart, I do this for some loved me but for a moment.

"My Holy Spirit is circling this earth and calling my bride to me, calling her gently, calling her to me. My love has kept her safe, hidden by me for a time such as this.

Now my beloved bride, come forth as I unfold you to the world, come for it is time for the Spirit and the bride to say, Come! You have been tried, tested, and found true. I will now *unfold* you to *enfold* and *entrust* you with greater power, for my Holy Spirit will strengthen you with a double portion of faith, for faith works by love. I have promised that you would do greater works, for I go before you, and the Enemy cannot and dare not touch you! I have reversed the curse for you by the shedding of my blood." (Gen. 3:14–15)

Again the Lord speaks: "For now you will *bruise* the enemy's *head*."

- *Bruise*: to break down by pounding; noun, a surface injury to flesh
- *Head*: the front or upper part of the body containing the brain, the chief sense organs, and mouth
- *Heel*: the hind part of the foot; one of the crusty ends of a loaf of bread

The Lord explains: "With your *heel* you will cause a contusion to Satan's flesh, which will cause sin to rise to the surface and expose him for who he is and those that serve him. He cannot hide from you, for you continually say, 'You are not my head, Satan,' and it will be as if you are *pounding him on the head with the crusty-hard end of an elongated loaf of bread*! For, beloved, I am with you as the living Word, the *Bread of Life*."

Did you laugh at this description, me two! The Lord makes me laugh all the time. By the way, the Lord would like to hear us sing happy songs with tears of joy instead of woe-is-me songs with tears of pain. Rejoice, church! We belong to the King of Kings and Lord of Lords, no matter our flesh shortcomings and the pain it inflicts in others and us!

The Lord continues: "Be encouraged, my beloved, for I too walk by faith, for only the Father knows the hour and the day of my second coming and my heart is stirred by the signs of the times and your nearness. Let us encourage one another, my beloved. Draw close to me, and I will draw close to you. My heart beats fast in great anticipation of my return for you!

"My good seed (love-word) is planted in my beloved's fertile ground by the Holy Spirit, for it descends from the Father. This seed is the origin of all truth, for I am the way, the truth, and the life, and no one comes to the Father but by me. Any other gospel preached is not of me. 'Seed faith' is not of me; it is a misnomer (a wrong or inappropriate name or designation), for faith is the substance of things hoped for, the evidence of things not seen. This is a ploy of the Enemy, a tactic intended to confuse and frustrate you, causing you to take your eyes off me and to focus on the prosperity promise of money in this world, which shall pass away. 'Oh if you knew me you know my prosperity is of a greater measure then the worlds for mine will never pass away in this life and last for eternity.

"My beloved will be made manifest, and I will provide and care for her every need, for I AM that I AM, her redeemer and we are betrothed soon to be wed. For I take care of my own. Pride and avarice is far from her, for she has been humbled under the mighty hand of God, and there are no other gods before her therefor she shall be exalted and crowed queen."

Once again, I am hearing a song, and it goes like this: "Open our eyes, Lord, so we might see Jesus." This song is ringing in my ears. We sang it in the Catholic Church. What a blessing! How sweet it is to serve our Lord. Sing *hallelujah* to our soon-coming King!

Tonight as I was praying (October 27, 2005), this came to my heart: Man is so busy fighting for first place that he misses the blessings before him, because the blessings are all in and through our Lord Jesus Christ. Without faith, it is impossible to please God; for man is prideful, and greed will always seeks for and covets the things of this world.

We have not, because we ask not, or we have asked amiss. Instead of asking for more of Jesus, the author and finisher of our faith, we ask for temporal things that fade away. Do you not know that he is in everything that is good and that everything ever made 'was made by him? You cannot have anything apart from him, and no good thing will he withhold from them that love him. When we pray and our prayers seem to be not, answered as we think they should be, we should confess like this: "I do not go by what I see, hear, or feel, but I go by every word that proceeds out of the mouth and heart of God-the word of God," instead of complaining!

I trust him. In addition, if we trust him, we will live with great contentment, no matter what state we find ourselves in; for faith is the substance of things hoped for, the evidence of things not seen. I still have prodigal children who have gone their own way, but I placed them in God's hands. I trust him with my grown up children, for he is the greater parent, thus releasing me to love, hope and serve him. I do not boohoo about it anymore, because I draw close to him and he never left me comfortless.

To me, the ultimate prosperity is to become more like Jesus. For if, we gain the whole world but lose our very souls, what good is the world's prosperity to us?

When I met Jesus, 'I fell head-over-heels in love with Him and I was transported from death into a new life. I could breathe pure air for the first time, like a newborn baby inhaling its first breath! Now born-again, I realize—for the first time in my selfish, self-centered life—that my sins 'are forgiven because I accepted Jesus as my Savior.

No matter what perils or heartaches befall me and mine, he will see us through them all. In spite of my faithlessness when I was growing up, he freed me—naturally and spiritually. Now my prayer is this: Please help me, Lord, to draw even closer to you, and as I do, free me from my selfish ways that give me license to habitual sin. For no matter how small the sin is, sin is sin, and it cannot be justified in your presence and willful sin separates us from you.

Please, my Lord, never depart from me, for I am helpless without you, lost and alone at best, even in a crowded room, without you. The glimmering lights of this world pale next to your glorious light and your constant presence in my life. I bask and take comfort in your promise that nothing shall ever separate me from your love.

My Lord has remained faithful to me when I stumbled on the way; he just picked me up dusted the dirt off me. He encouraged me to continue to follow him, saying, "Do not give up, my precious one!" My earthly parent was not so tolerant of me, nor was I of my own children. Beloved, you can be a parent and not know your own children. In the same way, you can be a Christian and not know the Lord; for to know him is to love him. Then, as you know him, you will obey him when he says, "If you love me, feed my sheep." By the way, if you obey God, all hell will break out against you! Once I was young, and now I am old and now beating the Enemy on the head with the Bread of Life.

We all suffer much for our lack of knowledge of the word our Lord Jesus, and we will perish for the lack of a vision of him, which is the only way to overcome. The Enemy can still come in to kill and destroy us if we take our eyes off Jesus, because only the truth of our Lord Jesus sets us free. My Catholic mother prayed for her children. She accepted Jesus Christ as her Savior, and God answered her prayers, for he saw her heart! Beloved, denominations are not the answer. We have been scattered for a season, and we 'will be united for his reason. The name of that reason is Jesus, the name that is above all names: Emmanuel, "God is with us."

I know some will disagree with me. Just remember that the Father, Son, and Holy Spirit never cause division. The Enemy can only divide us when we agree with him! Remember, beloved church, there is only one good seed, and that is our Lord Jesus Christ. Any other seed that man is trying to plant in your heart (field) is a lie, and it will wither and die on the vine and be cast into the fire and burned! Jesus said, "And I, if I be lifted up from the earth, I will draw all men unto me...John 14:6" Beloved, if we proclaim to the world that Jesus is Lord, the Holy Spirit will do the drawing.

Take care what seeds you plant, for they will multiply and eventually perish. Jesus said that he is the only good seed, and his seed (love-word) will never perish but produce everlasting life. Whatever you sow, you will reap, whether it is corruptible or incorruptible. You must choose whom you will serve: God (truth) or mammon (lies).

Beloved, in this hour, Jesus is stretching forth his hands toward his church, saying, "Behold my mother and my brethren! For whosoever shall do the will of my Father, which is in heaven, the same is my brother, my sister, and mother... Matt. 13: 49-50"

Jesus said he is the only good seed (gospel), and the enemy sneaks in by the cover of night and plants his own seeds, tares, or lies (false gospel) among the wheat. Nevertheless, be of good cheer, for Jesus has overcome the world, and it is darkest before the dawn. "Before the daystar arises in our hearts...II Peter 1:19–21 "I Jesus have sent mine angel to testify unto you these things in the churches. I am the root and the offspring of David, and the bright and morning star...Rev.22:16"

Jesus explained the purpose of the parables. "And the disciples came, and said unto him, Why speakest thou unto them in parables? He answered and said unto them; because it is 'given unto you to know the mysteries of the kingdom of heaven, but to them it is not given...please read all of...Matt. 13: 1-17 for a greater understanding.

Now rejoice, beloved, for he has not turned you away! The ones who preach the good news know the mystery of the gospels; but those who preach what is false do not know, and they pervert the gospel, for it is not, given to them, to understand it.

Jesus explained throughout the parables the stages and strategies of the Enemy: to steal, kill, and destroy the Word of God that 'was planted in our hearts. This Word of the kingdom is the proclamation that Jesus is the only begotten Son of God, who was 'crucified died, was buried, and rose on the third day. Any other bread is leaven false gospel, for Jesus is the bread of life, our blood sacrifice. In addition, remember that a little leaven (evil) goes a long way (Matt. 13:33). After teaching in parables, Jesus sent the multitude away.

No amount of money or things of this world could give me what I needed. Only my Lord Jesus could fill the empty void I felt all my life. The Lord wrapped me like a newborn baby in His love, and I cried out for more of His love. I had an unquenchable thirst, like a baby for mother's milk, and the Holy Spirit fed me the milk of the Word.

Then, as I matured, I began to hunger for the meat of the Word, constantly hungering after the Lord. I cried with longing as I learned of him, and my desire for him was without measure. I cried, "Please help me, my Lord, to contain the love you have given me. The more love you give me, the more of you I want! He said, "You are not to keep my love to yourself, Evelyn. You have to give it to others, and then I will fill you up with more to overflowing."

My thirst was unquenchable and my hunger insatiable, but then the Lord said this to me: "Your cup is overflowing with my love for you so that you can fill others. Now, go feed the hungry with the bread of life and the thirsty with the water of the Word. Go to the lost, hurting, and dying of this world, for if you love me you will feed my sheep."

I cried again, when I heard him say this; for I had very little education and no teaching skills, for I had a learning disability caused by a bad head injury to my temple after a fall. As a child, I found it hard to understand what 'was taught! However, it is no small thing that the infilling of the Holy Spirit gifted me to write poems, and I have been sharing them with others ever since—feeding my Lord's sheep in my own small way. What an unmerited gift he has bestowed on me, with the dual pleasure of sharing him with others, for we are 'all called to be a blessing to others.

The song of my soul comes from Matthew 25: My Lord, I hunger and thirst after you. When I was hungry, you gave me meat: the bread of life. When I was thirsty, you gave me drink: the living waters of your Word. When I was a stranger, you took me in, adopting me into your family. I was naked, and you clothed me with your love. I was sick and dying in my sins, and you healed me with your blood that now covers me, cleansing, healing me from all unrighteousness, keeping me from the wrath of God.

I was in prison, and you visited me—a prisoner bound and shackled to this world of sin—and you set me free from the law of sin and death. I weep, Lord, at what I am hearing from you. Yes, my Lord, I was naked, spotted, and riddled with sin, and you clothed me with your love, covering me with your life-giving blood. Then, if this was not enough, you filled me with your precious Holy Spirit, making me the temple of the Holy Spirit, who is now my own personal mentor and teacher. He is gently leading and guiding me to become more like you, Lord. What a privilege you have given me: now *accepted* into the beloved and *adopted* into your royal family. It is just as Paul explained in his epistle to the Romans.

Even with this great love, I have for you, my Lord and king, I cannot boast. For without you first 'loving me, as you do' I could not have loved you as I do. Because of your blood sacrifice, my destiny is now assured, and one day I will rule and reign with you for eternity. It is truly unmerited, this great grace that you have bestowed on me and on all those who believe and truly love you.

"I charge you, O ye daughters of Jerusalem, by the roes, and by the hinds of the field, that ye stir not up, nor awake my love, until he please" (Song 2–7).

My beloved Lord, my love quicken, revive, refresh us with the fire of your love, if it please thee.

"And the Spirit and the bride say, Come" (Rev. 22:17a). The Lord says that he will come quickly (Rev. 3:11, 22:7)

Some definitions are helpful. *Quicken* means "to come to life, revive to arouse, stimulate curiosity (e.g., quicken my interest), to increase in speed." *Hasten* means "to show vitality as growing or moving." (See Song 2:7; Isa. 60:1; Matt. 13:43.)

When freed from the tares, "then shall the righteous shine forth as the sun (sons) in the kingdom of their Father. Who hath ears to hear, let him hear what the Spirit is saying to the churches.

I want to thank God for the Catholic Church for this is where my spiritual life began. I am sure that my praying mother and Mormon grandfather Peter Young, whom I never met, prayed for me. My husband and I accepted Jesus Christ as our Savior while watching Billy Graham's crusades on TV, and while I visited a neighbors church a visiting evangelist prayed with me for the infilling of the Holy Spirit. Many other Christians in different denominations have blessed me I thank God for all of them. However, as a young Christian I 'was buffeted with false doctrine and the enemy went on a rampage to kill, steal, and destroy from me and mine.

I became discouraged and confused I went back into the world thinking what I experienced was not true! For the Love I experienced when I fell in love with Jesus was not in the churches I visited.

Beloved, we are to try every spirit to see if it is of God. We are not to judge one another; the Lord will do that when we all stand before him, when he judges the living and the dead. Remember that we are all flawed at best, and the tares are still among us; there is no one good but the Father. I do not fear what man can do to me, but I have a great, reverential fear of the highest Father God.

In Retrospect

This book is about my personal encounter with my Lord, Jesus Christ, God's only begotten Son, who is the living, loving, patient, most kind and gracious Son whom the Father has given to all who believe in him. Now is the time to honor Jesus as we learn of him, for he truly came to give us life and that more abundantly. As we live and have our being in and through him, the abundance of him in our lives will increase, and faith will abound in us.

Once again, I will say that Jesus is the only good seed; when planted in our fertile ground, it will produce after its own kind. Then he will come forth in 'his entire glorious splendor into our lives, where some of us will produce thirty-fold children and some a hundred-fold. This is the test of our intimacy with our Lord. Intimacy with Jesus has nothing to do with the sexual feelings we experience in our natural state. Jesus instructed me to embrace with his love, which I described in a poem the Holy Spirit gave me: "Love Is the Key."

When I embraced with his love, I got in trouble in the church, because too many were walking in the flesh and not the Spirit. They began two falsely accuse me of all manner of evil. Since I was a widow, they accused me of wanting their husbands—young or old, it did not matter—it got crazy. They could not see that I was married to Jesus, and this frustrated me. When I realized what was happening, I left, for I choose to obey God rather than man. I believed that he would fix what was wrong in me—or in them. I knew enough of the Word to know that the Enemy was out to steal, kill, and destroy the Word from within me, and the persecution was relentless as long as I was walking in his love. I am seventy-one years old now, and the Enemy is still at it! He is so stupid and still trying to marry me off. Yet I have grown in wisdom and now know not all will receive the Lords embrace free from the flesh, at first I thought it was because I was young and attractive but that is not the case anymore, it is the Lords love they fear not mine.

It is time to grow up, church, and get your head out of the Enemy's gutter and exposes the Enemy for who and what he is: a liar. Let us embrace one another in the beauty of His holiness with the Lord's most holy love. Moreover, if we have sin issues, we need to repent and freed from them. However, please do not refuse the embrace of the Lord Jesus Christ, for he is supposed to be in each of us, and his love helps us to get over ourselves For greater is he, who is in me, then he, who is in the world.

Intimacy with Jesus filtered by his word the Holy Spirit, purifying us for the Lord's use and presence, we become holy for his use. It is all about bringing a harvest of children into the kingdom of God, not about us in the church. We have his Holy Spirit with us, who tills the soil of hardened hearts; we are not, left alone a banded to tend the world's soil. The Holy Spirit makes the hearts pliable in his hands, remolding and reshaping us into the image of God's only begotten Son.

We must yield the field of our wills to 'be cultivated by the Holy Spirit for he is the only one who can plant the good seed (word) in our hearts. Just as the Holy Spirit planted Jesus in Mary's womb so shall his seed be planted into our spiritual womb so Jesus can come fourth we two must say as Mary did let it be according to your word! Man is full of duplicity, disguising his true intentions by deceptive words or actions. We must study to make ourselves approved workers unto God so we can try every spirit to see if it is of God.

For God allows the tares—the weeds and false words—to grow among the wheat, and the Holy Spirit tenderly takes care that the tares do not choke the wheat. Do you think the pure Word of God—the Father's only begotten Son, the good seed, Jesus, who was cultivated and planted in your heart by the Holy Spirit,—could ever be destroyed? My answer to this question is never, never, never, and forever never.

The Word of God is now alive in my heart because of the Father's only begotten Son, who died and resurrected. He is the only good "seed" we should be planting. Now, because we are no longer of this world but are children of the kingdom, we can sow or speak the Word of God, in and out of season, for it is always planting season in God's kingdom. The pure Word sets the captives free. Now sow to the Spirit, not the flesh, and scatter abroad in their hearts the Word of God, for the Holy Spirit sows to man's spirit, and the Enemy sows to man's flesh.

Children of the Wicked One are sowing tares to the flesh, and they will reap corruption. Some twist the Word to further their own agendas. The Enemy counterfeits, because he cannot create after his own kind, for he was and 'is not created in God's image and likeness. Because of this fact, the Enemy hates man and needs man to create for him to further his kingdom, so he confuses man in order to use him.

Please read-Matt.13:34–46 and 'be blessed, because the Lord knows who the "pearl of great price" is. She is the one who does the will of her Father. She gives her all to him in order to fellowship in his suffering in order to have a deeper knowledge of him and to surrender every area of her life to him. Thus, the Holy Spirit reveals what is not of him, even as he teaches her to love others as herself, unconditionally. This lesson will continue until his righteousness shines forth in her as the sun (Son) in the kingdom of their Father.

Jesus has become everything to me. The moment I heard him say, "I will never leave you or forsake you," this truth became alive in me. I realized that he was the only one who truly loved me, for he was God, who would never lie, point a finger, accuse, bear tales, or backbite against me. He just accepted me the way I was: a big mess, a sinner, but now covered by his blood and thereby shielded from the wrath of God. Jesus knew that one day his beloved, will be without spot or wrinkle, would glorify him and the Father, for the Holy Spirit will cleans and purified her, (Eph. 5:27)

The truth 'will be perfected in us as we live by faith and mature in the Lord. The Father has promised that he will complete the good work he has begun in us—not by power or by might, but by his Spirit, the Lord said. This truth generated great hope and joy in me, because I began to understand that I was part of his beloved bride, and she was a many-membered body of the Father's making. She is his divine puzzle handpicked by the Father for his Son who knows where each of us belongs in the body. He places us where we belong in this life and in the next, for he went before us and prepares a place for us.

When I read the parable of the "pearl of great price," I began to understand the great price he paid for me, and I began to search for his bride but could not find her. Father God is the only one who knows her heart—who and where she is—and he will begin to assemble the puzzle, drawing them all together under one head: God's only begotten Son. God allowed Saul to scatter the bride abroad, and she went everywhere in order to preach the Word. Nevertheless, God turned what the Enemy meant for evil into good, and from Saul came Paul.

As I studied the Word, I began to experience who God was and how very much he loves us. His omnipotence, the infinite power of his love, began to heal my body, mind, soul, and spirit—not as the world heals but only as God can from the inside out. There was nothing natural about this healing process. It progressed as I yielded my will to him. You cannot understand this healing unless you experience it for yourself, and then you cannot explain it, because it is all about his all-encompassing, consuming love that passes all understanding. We are a work in progress, and we are, truly transformed from glory to glory to be his crowning glory. We are to be his greatest achievement, his beloved wife soon to be the crowning glory of her husband, Jesus Christ, and the whole earth was full of God's glory from the beginning. The Lord prophesies everything good into being by his Word, and the Enemy cannot stop it (Matt.16:17–18).

God's ways are so much higher than our ways. My beloved Lord has become everything to me—more than a father, mother, husband, or children. He is a friend that sticks closer than a brother does. He became everything to me in its purest, most holy form. I now know why we have to forsake all to follow him; it is because we do not know how to love as he loves.

My mind and spirit is, now opened to understand why I fell so short in loving others—and why others fell so short in their love for me. So much pain and sorrow, all the ills of the world, have come from lack of love. "The only way we can give love—unselfish, complete, and holy—as He does, is to draw close to him. Then we will decrease, and he will increase. The truth is simple, and it will set you free.

As a woman of faith, I do not go by what I see, hear, or feel. This is a very good thing, for I would have given up on myself a long time ago; there are times even now when I want to give up. The hardest thing for me to do is this: to keep myself separate from the world because I am in it but not of it, as a human I 'am bombarded with temptation every day.

With TV, movies, radio, media, computers, and all kinds of handheld gadgets, we have instant access to anything and everything that tantalizes the flesh or keeps us from thinking or choosing for ourselves. It amazes me how evil and corrupt man can become when left to his own *devices*. (This is not a pun; it is in the word of God: Acts 17:29; Jer. 18:12. Please be sure to read the context around these verses in Acts 17:22–34 and Jeremiah 18:1–23.)

After you read these chapters, pray that we will humble ourselves and that the Father will heal our land and will have mercy and send a revival. For I see judgment all around and on the horizon. As I understand how high the stakes are for all of us, I begin to tremble, because many are floundering in the church. They are going the way of the world, and many in our families are not, saved. However, I must remind you that his ways are higher than our ways, and what he has promised, he will do. Beloved, cling to Him, for he is God, the living Word, and there is only one comforter: the Holy Spirit...most men will only speak platitudes, to try to comfort.

'We are blessed because he is faithful, and we are able to use modern *devices* to download the Bible and to hear the Word twenty-four hours a day if we choose. This is just one example of how God turns things around for us. What the Enemy means for evil, God will turn to good for those that love and trust in him. Our weapons are not carnal but mighty through God to the pulling down of strongholds.

He is calling us to come away with him and learn of him, for he is not a hard taskmaster. He will meet you where you are. He desires intimacy with his beloved, because he wants you to know him, as he really is this seems a reasonable request from the groom to the bride.

I will share with you my way of holding on to him: I say, "I will not let go until you bless me, Lord. I know all blessings 'are fulfilled in and through you, so I am holding on to you, Jesus, with both hands and feet, no matter what I see, hear, or feel. This is not so easy to do anymore, Lord, for I have gained a few pounds since I fell in love with you. Besides, from this height— compared to the depths I came from—I would be a fool to let go of you now, splat!

It would be for me if I let go." Yet the Lord continues to assure me that his burden is light, and he will not let go of me…this 'is called blessed assurance.

Faith

This book is an ongoing, intimate story of my journey into my Lord and Savior's arms, and my journey has just begun, for I am still a work in progress. This is just a prelude, for the best is yet to come.

Now, look up, church! We are all empty and unfulfilled without him. In this lonely world, there are so many who are unsatisfied, lost, and alone. They stuff their lives with sex, drugs, money, and entertainment but when they come down from whatever high they are on, they just crash and will burn naturally and spiritually they are lost; they just do not know why—yet! This is where the church is supposed to step in with the truth by reflecting a more sure way of glory instead of the world's glory. Sadly, we have fallen very short, for the church is 'now infected by false doctrine and the world's glory oozing from every pore with the prosperity of the enemy's lies.

Beloved church, do not despair. Trust in God alone, and he will never let go of you and yours. Just believe in him! He has made a way of escape, and he is well able to take care of his own. We must remember that we live by faith and not by sight (Gal. 2:20–21). Our vision not impaired by this world's glory.

For those who believe that the world will supply their every need, there is a rude awakening waiting for them. Their vision has been, impaired and disabled by false words. The beautiful, pure, perfect vision I have is of Jesus and His kingdom. By faith and the purity of his Word, I will never perish for lack of a vision, because the world shall pass away, but His word will never pass away. My focus is on him, for I love him.

I will never perish for lack of a vision, for I only have eyes for him and not you false teacher. My eyes 'are fixed on him. My heart belongs to my Lord, and a most lovely sight is he. I love you, my King (Songs 5:16; Ps. 57:7–11). Yep, you guessed it. I am in love with Jesus.

I want to note here that I take exception to someone who said that he went to heaven and comforted Jesus because Jesus said that no one loved Him. This is a lie. Remember that Lucifer is the prince of the air—*hot* air. He has a false light and is the father of all lies. That false light was on this person when he supposedly came back, all aglow, from Jesus' presence, and people who were around him when he came back were supposedly "slain under the power of God." I do not doubt that this was Lucifer's doing, for he is an angel of light—and a counterfeiter, a jokester, and trickster like this little disciple.

Therefore, with the authority Jesus has given us in his Word (Matt. 16:19, 18:18), I now bind thee to your lies, you false preachers, teachers, and prophets on earth, and so shall you be bound in heaven. And whatsoever I loose on earth shall be loosed in heaven; therefore, let the truth of Jesus' holy Word be loosed once again on earth, as it is in heaven, to set us free.

Now, come away with me, and read on as I share what Jesus has done and is doing for me, as he remolds and reshapes my heart, making it pliable in his hands for his use. This is for his honor, glory, and praise, for I live for him and have my being in him. There is nothing' I want that is apart from you, my Lord and King, in this life or the next. I adore and worship you beyond what I can express. Help me, Holy Spirit, for I am not a teacher—just a woman, who loves you and wants to share the love you have given me.

Beloved, I could easily testify of the sins that were committed against me and the sins that I have committed against others. However, why should I? We are all born into sin; we are all sinners, no matter our station in life—rich or poor bond or free. We are all born with sin imprinted into our lives, and playing the "blame game," saying that someone else made us do those things, is a waste of time. This is my testimony: God set me free from the law of sin and death through the transfusion of his Sons' blood I 'now am covered by his D. N. A. "Devine Nature and Authority."

This I know, that the sins of the fathers have continued since Adam and Eve fell from God's grace and Eve gave birth to Cain and Abel. It soon became evident that Cain was jealous of Abel, for he killed him. Every sin ever conceived by man came from our ancestors, and we just continue to pass their sins along, from one generation to another. No matter how hard we try to curtail sin, it will never go away.

Because of the sin that is in our DNA, children will continue to be born into sin, deformed both naturally and spiritually, all of us subjected to the sins of the world. Some will be born with Cain's spirit and others with Abel's the only hope we have for the world to change is through Jesus.

This cleanup process continues in me, as I yield to the Holy Spirit, by the washing of the water of the Word. I will decrease as I confess my habitual sins before him and desire to be more like him. All the bad, evil 'that has happened to me and mine and to the world is because of the accumulation of sins of all humanity in this world not because God lets it happen but because all of us—even the earth itself—are a product of the fall of Adam and Eve. We serve a good God, who loves us so much that he made a way to free us from our sins, even when there was no way, by sending his only begotten Son. Sin will continue to affect all humanity until Jesus comes back for us, then there will be a new heaven and a new earth, and all things will become new (Rev. 22:1–21).

Sin has a snowball effect. It starts as a little white snowball—like a cuddly little baby at birth. As we roll down the mountain of life's circumstance that we are born into, we become a big—and then bigger—snowball/sinner. When the light of the gospel of our Lord Jesus Christ shines down upon us, it melts our hearts, washing our sins away. Then we pick ourselves up, dust ourselves off, and begin to run the race he has set before us, counting it all joy when we 'are persecuted for the gospel's sake. Note: This is not so easy for we like to-be liked!

The only way to be set free from this downward spiral is to accept Jesus Christ as our Savior. Then we will have the strength to endure the journey ahead, as we are washed with the pure water of the Word. All of us have two things in common: we are born, and then we die. Yet God so loved the world that he gave us a third choice his only begotten Son. Whosoever believes in him shall have eternal life. Because Jesus Christ shed his blood, we are now born of the Spirit as a new creation in Christ Jesus for eternity if we choose.

I hear so many people ask, "How can a good and loving God let all this evil happen?" The answer is that he does not let it happen. *We* do. Christians are at fault. We do not know him, because we do not draw close to him. Therefore, the world cannot see him as he really is. The entire world sees there reflection in us the so-called church today; we must humble ourselves under the mighty hand of God and come together in the unity of the Holy Spirit so that we will all reflect Jesus simultaneously.

This will happen when we reach a point in Christ Jesus where we do not care about being exalted, but want all the glory *for him*. Denominations get over your-selves and worship God. I am not telling you to dismantle but to assemble yourselves under Jesus and work together for the kingdom of God's sake. Denominations have divided God's people. Because of this, his people perish for their lack of a vision of him. Outside of the whole body, we are divided and unable to see. The eyes are the mirror of the soul, and as part of the whole body of Christ, we need to see clearly through his eyes, for Christ is the head of one body. If we continue to want to be first, we must remember that the first shall be last and the last first... humble is as humble dose.

Love one another and esteem others better than yourself. Judge not. Humble yourself under the mighty hand of God, and he will exalt you in due time, for soon he will judge the living and the dead. Again, I say, we are to try every spirit to see if it is of God. We are not to judge one another lest we 'be judged, because Jesus is the judge. Remember always that many 'are called, but few are chosen, and it has always been our choice—to choose Jesus or the world. Do you think this Scripture means that you are now part of some elitist group? No! You will have to humble yourself and come to him, transferring your will to *his* will being done. I say again that the gates of hell shall not prevail against his church.

There is no time to sit on the fence. You cannot serve two masters, having one foot in the kingdom of God and the other foot in the kingdoms of this world. Are you part of his beloved church that we will soon see at the unveiling?

This book contains the words of many years of my Lord speaking to me and repeating the same words in different ways to lead and guide me to the truth. His patience and love are without measure. I am not a preacher or teacher at this point, just a woman of faith in love with Jesus, taught by the Holy Spirit, entrusted with gifts and callings I do not deserve. Thank you, my Lord. I pray that all who read this book 'are blessed as you Lord have blessed me.

My "Priceless Pearl" Vision

Sometime after I experienced this open vision, I began to gather my writings together for this book. After much prayer about the title, I believe that *His Priceless Pearls Unfolding* was the answer to this prayer. Now, I go forward in spite of myself, for I have zero natural ability to write this book, as I shared in this introduction. I know that the ability is not from me but from he who lives in me, and I am very humbled as I stumble on this journey to write what is in my heart. God's Word often reminds me that nothing is too hard for the Lord, and then I am encouraged not to quit, knowing that, although my shortcomings will be evident, his glorious light will shine through in spite of the vessel he uses because I truly love him.

In addition, remember that pride should have no place in us. I now live by grace, and his grace is sufficient for me. Dear Father, Son, and Holy Spirit, if any good comes out of my life's testimony, please let it be to your glory, for we overcome by the blood of the Lamb and the Word of our testimony.

These personal pages are a minor-key expression, I believe, of my Lord's love for me and my love for him. It is as if I am sharing my personal diary. The Holy Spirit helps me to express myself in writing with musical overtones for his love is music to my ears, and my efforts fall so short. This is truly a fact. How can one express God's great love for us, a love that passes all understanding? 'His beautiful love has opened the floodgates of love in my heart expression and allowed his expressed love to flow from me—and with pen in hand, I will try.

Now, beloved, I pray that you will experience the Lord Jesus Christ's great love for you, if you have not done so already. Read on prayerfully, and you will see with your own spiritual eyes and hear with your spiritual ears that his holy love for us is personal. In his eyes, there is no one else like you or me. *Thank goodness*, you may think. Humbly, now, I summit this book into his safekeeping, forever proclaiming, "His kingdom come, his will be done on earth as it is in heaven, amen."

I pray that this book encourages you, for it is a product of the Holy Spirit leading and guiding me into the truth— the living Word of God, my Lord Jesus Christ, who is the fulfillment of the Word of God from Genesis to Revelation. Now, beloved of God, bask in his love, always remembering that any promise or blessing you are waiting for can only, be fulfilled in and through him. Nothing apart from him is of any eternal value and all else will fade anyway.

My Little Testimony

As a child, raised in poverty and a broken family I used to cry out to God from the oddest places under the bed, in the closet or attic, or from the tallest tree, I could climb. I cried out, "Why am I here? I do not belong here. Take me back home to you, God." I was so lonely for him, before I knew him, and did not belong always out of place or was I accepted by anyone, I was the odd ball! I could not understand his plan, and I became upset and distant from him because I felt abandoned by him, as my earthly father had abandoned me. Yet whenever I sinned, I felt so tormented and hurt by whatever sin I had committed until I quickly repented. This feeling of unworthiness and a sin-filled life followed me into adulthood until Jesus set me free I was a big mess of confusion hurt, anger, and resentment! Until I read Rom. 8: 28, 30; Eph.1: 5

Now I know who I am, whom I belong to, and why I am here. I found out that it takes a lot of salt, sand, and tears to make a pearl for are we not to be the salt of the earth. How glorious is the Lord! He turns all the bad into good for those who 'are called according to his purpose. This is my story, the testimony of a woman who 'was terribly abused as a child and into adulthood, who was too busy flailing her arms about and pointing her finger at others, blaming them for her torment! I was lost and alone, drowning in self-pity, until I found out that Jesus, was my redeemer, and had been by my side all the time. My precious Lord had been waiting for me to calm down and hear his still, small voice telling me to get out of the boat and walk on the calm water's with him.

The definition of *calm* is: (1) a period or condition free from storms, high winds, or rough water, (2) the complete or almost complete absence of wind, or (3) a state of tranquility. The first poem I wrote was "The Storms of Life." I learned, beloved ones, that being still is an act of our will and that is one reason we are to give him are will.

It is most interesting to look back now at the year 1979, when my husband was in a fatal car accident. Just before the accident, I had the infilling of the Holy Spirit with the evidence of speaking in tongues. Then, in 1981, I began to write poems and other writings without any education or training to do so—and it showed, at first. In addition, I wrote, "This is the third day and third hour of my second coming," which was a personal, prophetic word I should never have shared, but I was young in the Lord and wanted everyone to rejoice with me and help me understand all that the Lord was saying to me. Boy was I in for a rude awakening. I have since repented for being so foolish, because some people will take what you share with them and make it their own, giving no glory to the Lord.

As a baby in Christ Jesus, I learned to obey through the things I suffered. Now I am old, and I am still learning through the things I suffer. My eyes are now completely on the Lord, believing and knowing that he is God. The poems came one after another—"The Storms of Life," "Pearl of Great Price," "Love Is the Key," "Heartbeat Away," and more—before I fell apart! Now it is 2012 and I am seventy-one years old (young) and praising God for his mercy that endures forever for it is no longer I that live but him.

Thank you, Lord, for your grace, mercy, and favor on what was my hurting, disjointed life. There was nothing and no one else in heaven or earth that could have taken me out of the miry clay I found myself in (Ps. 40:1–21). I often asked the Lord, "Why not heal me completely without my having to take medication or go to doctors?"

This was his response to me: "When you are weak, that is when I am the strongest in you. Will you yield to me for the gospel's sake?" Now, how could I argue with the living Word, when he spoke so simply to me from his Word that even I could understand it? This much I know: that all things *do* work together for good for those that love him weather I see hear or feel it. In addition, his beloved must be humbled in order to be exalted, that we to shall be resurrected. That he my Lord continued to use me, even though my disjointed, hurting life was obvious becoming a cause of disagreement with the enemy of my soul as he tried to make mincemeat out of me through all my shortcomings. Accusing me over and over again pointing out my unworthiness that I could do nothing right it was an echo from my past, the lie became obvious even to me for my anointing just increased as I decreased! Echoing his loving words to me come as you are, come unto me all you who are heavy laden and I will give you rest.

His ways are so much higher than our ways. I gave up trying to understand and stopped "kicking at the pricks." Now I just walk by faith—, which I was supposed to do in the first place. We have to experience him in order to know him the total length and breadth of him. We must submit to him, trusting in him with patient endurance in order to undergo change. This change happens in a twinkling of an eye, but it is not what *we* perceive to be a twinkling, for he is God and his ways are higher than our ways.

The word *patient* means "bearing pain or trials without complaint, showing self-control, and calm, steadfast, persevering." This does not sound like me yet. However, there is hope, for I am a woman of faith and I have a sense of humor because of the joy in my heart.

The beloved bride of Christ Jesus does not have to wait for her Lord's blessings, for he *is* her blessings; anything less than the promised fullness of him will not do (Matt. 5:1–16). Hear, all you heavens: the things of this world no longer have a hold on this bride, for she is wonderfully made fashioned and humble, a reflection of Christ. This is the promise I am really looking forward to for the body gathers where eagles fly (Matt. 13:24–30).

Some who claim to be one-hundredfold overcomers are in fact the tares among the wheat—worldly without remorse. Also, the spiritually unprepared (Luke 17:37) are vultures among the body. Yet in all this Christ's bride flies higher, higher, and higher above all the others, being content in the knowledge that one of her attributes is to fly like an eagle and see from a great height.

The bride of Christ is never, accepted, and always rejected by the Pharisees and Sadducees of her day. The Word tells us to be happy and exceedingly glad; for they, also persecuted the prophets in like manner—and great will be there reward- in heaven. This is my take on it—we live by faith in him to complete the good work he has begun in us. His beloved is different from others; 'she is led by the Holy Spirit and away from following the crowd, for she heeds the call of the two turtledoves, and she too will sacrifice her life for her Lord. She is now strong in spirit, filled with wisdom and his great grace (Luke 2:40).

Her faithfulness has advanced her forward into a rank and dignity that no other will possess; her loving trust guides her to her King. Therefore, she will continue to increase in great grace, maturing rapidly as the Holy Spirit leads her. Continually praying, studying to make herself approved as workers unto God, she obeys the Holy Spirit's prompting as he leads and guides her into the truth, thus advancing her above the world's high places of idolatry.

Now she holds her Lord's hand, for their union will soon, be, consummated when he returns, achieving complete spiritual perfection. She is now ready, for she sees her Lord and King with her spiritual eyes (Rev. 21:9–27). Glory radiates from her, for the Holy Spirit has prepared her. Now she waits patiently for her Lord and King (Ps. 73:1–28) to see him face-to-face with her natural eyes (Ps. 73:1-18; 1 Cor. 13:12).

She is confident, assured, and at peace, knowing that the natural and the spiritual will take place. They now have become one: no longer just a communion of remembrance of him but a perfect communion with him in his promised return for her, his second coming (1 Cor. 15:35–58). Always proclaiming this, I am confident that he will never leave me or forsake me. He will return.

Many are called, but few are chosen (Matt. 20:16). My comment here is that we all have free will to choose to accept or reject Jesus. It is our choice to heed his call. Now up, up they go, for eyes have not seen nor ears heard what God has prepared for those that love him (1 Cor.

2:1–16). Holy matrimony is her calling; predestined from the foundations of the world is this union.

Holy Spirit, sweet dove of Christ Jesus, teacher of all that is holy, you are the Father's great joy unspeakable to be hold, full of Father God's glory, as his only begotten Son. You have taught his bride to see through your eyes, piercing the darkness, dispelling it with the truth of your nobility and excellence, achieved in her through the purity of her Lord's intersession.

Because of her Lord's faithful intercession for her, she now reaches for the mark for the prize of the high calling in Christ Jesus.

Her eyes see past the visible into the invisible. She has doves' eyes, like her beloved in Song of Solomon 6:1–3, and she looks right through the natural into the spiritual, tearing down the strongholds of the Enemy. She is as terrible as an army with banners, is his beloved. The banner over her is love (Songs 2:4), for she is led, not driven, by her Lord. She is committed to pleasing him, soaring where angels fear to tread, even to the throne of grace where Father God dwells. By faith, his love will be her crown.

The Vision Begins

My vision unfolded as I lay down for a nap. I do not remember falling asleep, but I found myself soaring up, up past what I perceived to be the Garden of Eden. How I knew it was that garden, I do not know. I just did. I was holding on to my beloved Lord Jesus' arm. I was very peaceful, breathing in the breathtaking fragrance of my Lord and King as we ascended hand-in-hand to the eternal throne of grace. Again, I will say that I just knew him, and where we were going as we ascended up!

It was a sensual, holy place, a place of pure and holy perfect love with pulsating lights everywhere. A cloud of glory surrounded us as we advanced forward. Holy, vibrating sounds of praise ignited through space and time, with thunder and lightning is everywhere. As we drew near the throne, we heard a thundering voice saying, "She has become a fine-tuned instrument, soaring beyond the Garden of Eden into a dimension of power and majestic holy grace, a royal and joyous place where there is no more sorrow or pain, for my Son will wipe away her every tear."

Then I heard again this booming voice saying, "You have been vindicated, avenged, and defended. You are justified, forgiven from all sin, and you now attain all rights to assert my authority upon the enemy. For you have reached the mark for the prize of the high calling in my Son, Christ Jesus, my beloved one, rejoice!" Then a soft, musical voice vibrated around me, saying, "Yes, you are chosen but not yet installed, beloved of God. There's much to do yet, much to do."

As this vision or dream continued, the Lord took my hands and placed them on each side of his face as he looked at me, and all I could see were his flaming, love-filled eyes that left me trembling and breathless. Then he spoke softly to me: "It is not time yet, my beloved, for this is the time for the Spirit and the bride to say, 'Come up higher to the unmerited throne of grace.'"

As I heard him say this, my heart sank, for I knew then that there was still much for me to do. I was disappointed but not daunted, for my desire was to please my Lord.

Suddenly I knew what to do. "Yes," I replied. "I will encourage the bride to come up higher into this glorious, unmerited, holy place." Holding my Lord's hand, I knew he would never leave my side, never forsake me on the journey ahead.

Hearing him say, you forsook all to follow me even your precious children. As I looked down from his tender gaze with tears streaming down my face, the Lord used his hand to wipe the tears from my face. I smiled up at him, and there was a soft radiant glory surrounding us as he embraced me. I said, "I love you, and I live to please you, my Lord and King it was like my whole being was melting into his embrace."

He spoke again, but his voice was like a song, embracing me in waves of holy love. He sang, "My gentle bride-Queen of grace, my bride, is willing to go forth, exuding God's love from every pore, healing with her beloved's love. My beloved will endure the journey ahead." Suddenly, I was holding a baby in my arms. He explained, "This is the promise of our combined anointing that you carry in your arms."

Then we began to descend, walking in place, for we were now one with each other. As we proceeded forward, he caressed my hand and lifted it to his face, speaking softly and so tenderly that I can still hear these words vibrating from him: "Yes, she will do this for me." I heard his heart pounding so hard that I knew all heaven could hear it.

Then he spoke to me in vibrating tones, in octaves, in musical notes so clear and perfect. He said, "My beloved, the price I paid for you is of no value compared to your worth to me and to my kingdom, for I would do it again—

time and again without end—for you. Pearl of Great Price is no longer your name for you are my destiny, destined to be my one and only queen, my Priceless Pearl. Nothing will ever, or *can* ever, separate you from me, for your faith, your great love for me, has secured you to me. Be at peace, for you are now complete in me."

Then he proclaimed, "I AM that I AM" called Wonderful, Counselor, Mighty God, the everlasting Father, Prince of Peace. Yea and I am the Almighty, the Alpha and Omega, the beginning and the end of all that was and will ever be-I am lasting to everlasting your king of many crowns.

Now I officially declare to you my eternal love for you. You are a vessel of my power and my glory, for you now understand that I have given you power to bless, not curse, which works through forgiveness. For forgiveness is the catalyst of my love, propelling my love forward, setting the captives free and my love will never change. Now, my beloved go forth trumpeting my Word and setting the captives free. My Holy Spirit is with you, and I go before you."

Then I woke up and was so close to the edge of the bed that I nearly fell out of it! I wrote this vision, dream down with tears streaming down my face as soon as I got my bearings.

As I try to type this vision and put words to it, it is hard for me, because my heart hurts with longing to return to my Lord. My experience brings tears of joy to my eyes, for there are no words that could ever express what happened in this vision. This vision 'will be forever, imprinted into my very heart beat. In truth, I now know the meaning of the Scripture that says that for "we live, move, and have our being in him." I breathe in these words each day for just a moment, and they refresh me so I can go on.

This vision is exquisite droplets of the vision that floats up to my memory, refreshing me, repeatedly. The Holy Spirit revealed the height, depth, and breadth of him in the wonder of this vision, for so much happened in such a short time. As I tried to remember his face, all I could recall was a beauty not of this world brilliant, beautiful light emanating softly from his face, obscured by the pulsating glorious light that surrounded him, so close was he I felt his breath on my face.

I know this does not make sense, but I saw him, yet I did not. I was there, but was I; it was a dream or a vision or both it was not confusion but a wonder! One thing I am sure of: it was not of this world and this vision has never left me. I was, transported twice, out of harm's way and this feels the same it leaves you shaking your head asking yourself did this just happen! I say to myself! *How can this be possible? How did this happen to me? Yet beloved this vision has never left me and it gives little me a purpose of sharing His great love for his bride Church.*

The Holy Spirit prompted me to look up the word *vista*. Then he said, "This vision is a *vista* of things to come: a vision that opens an extensive mental view over a series of years." Wow' huh! I will glean from these words for years to come. The Holy Spirit never leaves us wondering in the dark. He will explain if we ask him to, and I did. As I am concluding this writing, a Spanish song came on easy listening channel called "You belong to my Heart" a song that always brings tears to my eyes I know it was the Lord affirming this vision to me for he is beyond the romance of this world and meets our every need with his perfect love. I believe this vision is not mine alone; it is the power of his beloved church when we, are unite in him. Beloved ones, ten can put a thousand to flight, and two can put ten thousand to flight. (Lev. 26:8; Deut. 32:30; Ps. 91:7). Do the math, church; do the math.

I had this vision in 2005. It is now 2012, and now it is time to share it with you.

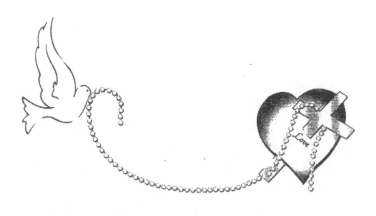

Chapter 1
Poems of Great and
Precious Promises

We 'are sealed with the Holy Spirit of promise.
—Matthew 10; Ephesians 3, 4, 5, 6; Isaiah 6:3

God's promises are *yes* and *amen*, which are fulfilled in and through his Son, our Lord Jesus Christ. "Great and precious are his promises." (II Pet. 1: 4)

- "If you love me, keep my commandments and I will pray the Father, and he shall give you another Comforter that he may abide with you forever." (John 14: 15, 16) now please read all of John 14.

- "Nevertheless, I tell you the truth; it is expedient for you that I go away: for if I go not away, the Comforter will not come unto you; but if I depart, I will send him to you." (John 16:7) Jesus 'was pledged on the cross and our eternal security is in him, the promised vow of our salvation.
- "For God so loved the world that he gave his only begotten son." (John 3:16). In this sacrifice, he laid down his life willingly, so that through him we might have everlasting life.
- "There is now no condemnation to them which are in Christ Jesus, who walk not after the **flesh**, but after the **Spirit**." (Rom. 8:1) now please read all of Roams 8,
- "And from Jesus Christ, who is the faithful witness and the first begotten of the dead, and the prince of the kings of the earth. Unto him that loved us and washed, us from our sins in his own blood, and have made us kings and priests unto God and his Father; to him be glory and dominion forever and ever." Amen (Rev. 1:5, 6) please read the rest of this first chapter of Revelation.

His promises are too many for me to mention here. I pray you read the "Word of God" with a greater understanding from Genesis to Revelation and you will truly be blessed dear ones. 'To him, be all the glory and dominion forever and ever. Amen

The Holy Spirit inspired me to draw the logo in closed in this chapter after I wrote "Pearl of Great Price," "The Storms of Life," "Love Is the Key," and "Heartbeat Away"— all to your glory, my Lord and King. I also want to thank the young woman who help me with the dove I finely placed on the Logo.

E. C.

Pearl of Great Price

(Matthew 13:45–46)

I gave everything I had to obtain a Pearl of Great Price.

You are that Pearl, my anointed bride; your love is mine.

For, beloved, such is the kingdom of heaven.

Rejoice in what you hear, my love, for I shed my blood at Calvary, and I, Jesus, would

Do it again 'time and again without end, for you.

The Storms of Life

(Matthew 8:23–27)

I see the storms of life whipping and lashing out at me, beating at the ship that I am in

Then I remember that I am not alone.

I walk over to the corner where Jesus is asleep, and I lie down next to Him, resting my head on His shoulder, trusting and believing in Him.

Then He speaks to the storm: "Peace, be still and know that I am God" (Ps. 46:10).

Comments

"The Storms of Life" poem, was given to a few people with the Scripture, Matthew 4:37–40, misprinted on it there is no such scripture. Please excuse this mistake. I have corrected it. Thank you, *E. C.*

Love Is the Key

(Matthew 5:43–48)

Embrace with my love.

Heal with my love.

Reach out, I say, to those who persecute and despitefully use you.

Reach out and pray for your enemies, for such as they, I died for.

Reach out, I say. No greater love is there than to lay down your life for your brother.

Reach out, speak love, and not hate; a friend then will I make from an enemy that hates.

For love is the key to resurrection power from me-(revival).

Show the world, my disciples, for one test did I leave:

To-love one another, as I love you.

Reach out to one another and forgive.

For how can you save the world if your brother is lost?

Do not judge them. Love them.

Reach out, my beloved, reach out to one another, and be like me.

For love reveals the truth and the truth sets you free.

For surely persecution 'must come but not by me (Matt. 5:43–48).

Heartbeat Away

My love my life, my soon-coming king; I bask in your presence. I adore you my life; I hear your heartbeat. You are so close to me. My love, how can I express what I feel for you? Help me, please' blessed Holy Spirit, with the words to convey to my Lord and King what my heart longs to say. I wonder if there are words that will reveal the depth of your love for me and my love for you.

I long to 'hold you, my King hear me' please, my love: Never depart from me. Give me the grace. I pray, to be what you want me to be, oh precious Holy Spirit. Please prepare me for my Lord and King.

For without your love, I am nothing. There is only hope and grace in thee. Oh, how I long for you.

Do you hear this longing in my heart for you? It is so overwhelming. I call for you to come close, yet when you do, my Lord, I am undone by your beauty yet fulfilled in the paradox of your beauty for it is holy and peels away all layers of worldly desires replacing them with a longing for you and you alone.

Sweet rapture do I sense, my Lord and King, as your breath caresses my cheek. Sweet hyssop and myrrh touch my senses. You are but a breath away, a heartbeat from me. I love you, my life.

The Lord responds to his bride:

My bride, do not despair, for I am with you. My longing for you is beyond measure, beloved of mine. Draw close into my arms for I hear you, my bride, I hear your cry.

Never doubt that I AM near to you. My beloved, you are grace in motion, a sweet mixture of love and devotion; your beauty transcends space and time. You are of great worth and value to me, and my kingdom your value is beyond measure, my precious bride.
Note: this is my revised version of "Heartbeat Away"

Heaven-Sent

(Matthew 6:19–12; Isaiah 45:3)

Hi, Mom and Dad' did you know I was sent from a crib in heaven?

Where I was waiting for you, I played with Jesus and baby angels.

God said I am your special treasure, sent from the throne room above to grace your life with joy, peace, and love, a precious jewel to polish and buff till I sparkle and shine just like you.

I am so glad; I am so glad God sent me to you.

Comment 12/5/12

I want to make it clear that the baby angles that I refer to in "Heaven Sent" are my perception of precious baby-aborted angles that are playing with the babies that are waiting to be born into the world. For some people are so puffed up with their bible thumping ways they will not give me poetic license. Can I prove this is scriptural-no! Can you prove it is not! Do you not call your children and grandchildren your little angles I do believe, that anyone who is in heaven, will be idle, but will joyfully work God's will in the kingdom of their God? For evil, even the residue of it cannot stand in his presents. Yes, I believe we have baby and child angles in heaven that 'were taken from us to soon and they are with the Lord in heaven.

I also want to make note hear that I remember that when our new president and our beautiful first lady went to England she was greeting two young beautiful black girls and she called them treasures! However, I thought how sad that the president and the first lady do not think our precious aborted babies 'are treasures and not even human yet, and it is ok to abort them. I pray they change their minds one day, my Lord, and with the power of their office do what they can to protect all the children. I just know that an apple seed is still an apple' if we nurture and protect it, it will grow and bear fruit of its own. God help us to see the beauty and possibilities and miracle of every human seed...black, white, yellow, red, pink bond or free they are all treasures, it is up to us to bring them up in the way they should go love and embrace the ones that are not. Remember love costs us nothing but commitment... this is the real physical cliff, we are in danger of falling off. God forgive us for musing over money' more than are angles.

This poem called "Heaven-Sent" has been an honor to share with others, for it has brought great joy to many. Below is a comment from one dear Christian woman with whom I shared this poem. This is not to boast but to bring all glory to the work of our Lord, Jesus Christ. If he can use me, dear ones, he can use anyone.

"Evelyn sent this poem to me as a gift for my granddaughter before she was born. It was then, and is still now, a favorite of mine. I love reading it to my granddaughter when I visit her. It was so touching, yet so true. Wish more people would listen to and live by the mighty words our Lord has given us (Matt. 6:19–12; Isa. 45:3). Thank you, Evelyn. -Juanita P."

Crushed for His Glory

(I love you and dedicate this poem to you, Donna F.)

A soft breeze came to me one hot summer day, like soft angel wings brushing my face. A little crushed doll was she. Her eyes lit up as we talked in the hot summer sun, a gentle, sweet love coming from her like soft droplets of fresh cool water on my face, clearing my weary mind, for I was tired.

As my mind cleared, I saw the beauty in this broken doll as I embraced her; the Lord's love overflowed, gently connecting us together, refreshing me for another day. This precious one was in her car, and before she left, I asked if I could hug her, not knowing she was a cripple until I embraced her. As she drove away, my heart rejoiced, for her brave countenance gave me hope for another day and very much humbled me. She did not realize what a blessing she had been until later.

This experience taught me that, when crushed, we could become sour grapes or pure, sweet wine. Her body had been broken down, fermented with the yeast of life's circumstances, yet the Lord has not forsaken her. He has blessed and purified her for his use in spite of this life-altering trial that changed her body and life but not her spirit, for she has faith that one day her body 'will become whole again. This precious one has become weak, not really understanding it all, so the Lord will live strong in her. Through the bitter cup she has swallowed, the Lord has saved the best wine for last (John 2:10).

Comments

There are many soldiers like Donna who have been torn and broken in body and mind through life's circumstances through natural wars and spiritual ones 'who choose through faith in Jesus, to be a light that shines in dark places. I salute you, dear ones, whatever battlefield you are in for you bring much glory to the Father, Son, Holy Spirit, and the kingdom of God...and some have paid the ultimate price laying there life down for their brother keeping us safe from harm's way they now reside in heavenly places with the Lord.

Unmerited Grace

The dew that covers my senses, obscuring the drought of this world, covers me like a blanket as I rest in the cool stillness of the night. As your Word washes over me, a whispering breeze of the Holy Spirit ignites the fire of your love. As your word pours over your body, a warmth and peace that passes all understanding cleanses and purifies us—body, mind, soul, and spirit—for your use.

This is a testimony of the Father's great grace in our life: I am helpless and greatly humbled by the unmerited, manifold grace you have bestowed on me. This gift 'was freely given and I have freely received it. Thank you, my beloved King, for this unmerited grace you have bestowed on all who truly believe in you (John 1:17; Heb. 4:16).

Sweet Hush

I sense a pause in my spirit as I wait on the Lord, not unlike the quiet just before the storm. In anticipation of great change, I sense in my spirit that it is like a pause in time as a clock that no longer ticks, ticks from one second to another. It is as if, I have been, suspended in this moment, one heartbeat away from my heart's desire, as if a place in my heart 'was closed before and now is open to a new beat.

This hush, this stillness is greater than anything I have ever experienced. It is a shaking of my whole body, mind, soul, and spirit without movement. As I think about how this can be, I foresee a great change, and calm has overtaken me. The silence is almost deafening. It is as if death has come and gone, and I am caught' in between two worlds like a fish out of water, unable to breath in the open air.

However, I am at peace in this state, for it is no longer I live but Christ. Dead, yet alive, no longer am I thrashing about; trying to find my place in the beloved, for my place is in Christ Jesus. He is my sanctuary, my refuge, and I am his temple, his, and only his exalted place, because of his love for me and his blood that covers me. I am, 'greatly humbled by this and am now content, am trusting in him.

E. C.

For where he leads, I just follow a new path he has set before me.

Kaleidoscope of Perfect Love

My heart is bursting with love's first light. It is exploding everywhere inside of me like waves of the Father's holy glory. It is a kaleidoscope of mirrors reflecting glittering, glowing embers of his only begotten Son's holy light. As this light penetrates through my life, it has redeemed me from the law of sin and death. This is the height, depth, and breadth of his grace, mercy, and compassion for us, his endless love.

This is, and was, his passion on the cross for us, and as the Lord lay down his life, his reflective light first penetrated, piercing the Father's heart, and tearing the veil in the temple. It became perfect love manifested in the flesh, destroying the work of the Enemy. Now, beloved, his love in us and through us 'will be fulfilled, as we love one another. Then, soon as we come face-to-face with him, we will become just like him.

When he comes back for us, we will no longer have to live by faith, for 'we will. be changed *by* his glory *into* his glory *for* his glory! For faith is the substance of things hoped for, the evidence of things not seen. In seeing him, we become just like him, for the wife reflects her husband and the wife is the glory of the husband.

His perfect love cascades in and through all who love him, for they will have forsaken all to follow him. This will cause unity of the Spirit, manifesting his perfect love in his body, and this perfect love casts away all fear, for fear has torment. Time without end will this be, as we willingly drape our wills like a strand of pearls over the cross. The precious Holy Spirit holds on to us, gently preparing us as a many-membered body transformed by the power of his resurrection. The fellowship of his sufferings are made conformable unto his death (Phil. 3:10), as we are predestined to become the pearl of great price and one in Jesus (Matt. 13:45–46).

This kaleidoscope of perfect love will cause waves of God's holy glory to wash over us, presenting us to the Prince of Peace and forever passing in and through us to renew us. For behold' old things have passed away, and now all things have become new. This is God's eternal gift, a mystery fulfilled in his Son and through us. (1Cor. 11:7, Col 1:26–27)

God's holy love—forever living in, though, and among us—is his only begotten Son (1 Cor. 13:12–13).

Chapter 2
Vision of the Dancer

This vision of a dancer came to me after my vision of the "Pearl of Great Price," which is included in this book. As I was trying to read, my handwritten scribbling of this vision to transfer it into typing, tears again streamed down my face. This is what I saw.

I saw a man and a woman dancing across a stage, twirling around one another so fast they almost became a blur to my eyes. They were going so fast, they became one.

I saw in front of them a great stage, and there was a waterfall cascading down from above it. On both sides of the waterfall were bright, pulsating lights. As the dancers neared the end of the stage, a brilliant light enfolded them; it was Jesus, holding his hands out to them. I could see the scars on his wrists, and I heard him say, "There is neither male nor female in the kingdom of God, for I am the head of my body, the church. You are bone of my bone and flesh of my flesh."

As Jesus spoke these words to the dancers, they began spinning, spinning, faster and faster, drawing closer to him. When the dancers reached him, they embraced the Lord and disappeared into him, becoming one with him. As they did so, he said, "You are now one with the Father, Son, and Holy Spirit." Then I heard him say, "If you draw close to me, I will draw close to you, my beloved, and I will come to you quickly."

Comments

When this was over, waves of His holy love continued to wash over me, and I was, shaken to the bone, no bun intended very core of my being. In this vision he was saying, "All you have to do is come to me. For what good is the

E. C.

head without the body, and what good is the body without the head? Is not the wife the glory of her husband?

I tried to draw this vision of the dancer while it was still fresh on my mind. With tears streaming down my face, I felt so very inadequate; yet I was compelled to do so, and I did the very best I could. The woman's dress was of the finest linen, almost like transparent silk, and under each layer of the dress was a shimmering golden material. I never saw her face clearly, she was twirling so fast, and her beautiful, long hair was up in the air.

Then I heard the Lord say, "You are poetry in motion, a sweet mixture of love and devotion. You are my priceless pearl." My whole body was shaking as I shed tears of joy and thought, *why you would show a wretch like me this vision. No one will believe me.* I felt so very humbled and inadequate. It is a good thing I am a women of faith. I saw this vision in 2005.

Chapter 3
Gentle Songs of Love

E. C.

Spirit and the Bride

(Song of Solomon 1:2–17)

I am a very simple person in the natural therefore, my Lord simply speaks to me in simple terms so very softly, clearly, and personally, that it defies the imagination, filling my heart with his love. This is the hour, when the Spirit and the Bride will say, Come, come unto him, all you who are athirst, come. For whosoever will drink freely of the water of life will spend eternity with him and will never thirst again."

The Lord is calling, "Come and bathe in the river of life, I beseech you, my fair one. Come, come away with me, my beloved, and I will give you rest, for the time draws short. I love you beyond your comprehending my longing for you. I have been away, preparing a place for you. Eyes have not seen nor did ears hear what I have prepared for those that love me, for I am a master carpenter artisan with the greatest of skills.

Foxes have holes, and birds have nests, but the Son of Man has nowhere to rest his head (Matt. 8:20; Luke 9:58).

"Can't you see beloved church? We are his resting place, his Sabbath, and he is ours" (Matt. 8:20, Luke 23:56). Even the New Jerusalem coming down from God out of heaven, prepared as a bride adorned for her husband (Rev. 21:2, 7), cannot compare to what Jesus has prepared for his beloved bride. It is a mystery, a gift from the groom for his bride.

Velvet Peace Covers My Senses

At your embrace, my King, a peace enfolds me, extinguishing lost moments in time. The nuisance of life I still held on to, even as I walked through life, daydreaming and wishing for a love I could not find. Those lost moments were defeating me as I looked back.

I am now walking in harmony with God's will and am forever destined to walk as a woman of faith, never again to go by what I see, hear, or feel, forever remembering that faith works through love.

I first heard your sweet voice beckoning me out of the loneliness of the world's ways. I was in uttermost confusion, going round and round, always around the same bend in the road—until I heard your voice. Now a cover of heavenly velvet down envelops me; it is the security of your love. This comfort promises me that I will never, never be alone again, for your love has softly shielded me and enveloped me with your nearness. A peace has overtaken my lonely life, erasing the past and all its bondage.

My loneliness was a symptom of sin, sins I committed and sins others committed against me. Now I am forgiven and free to forgive others and myself. There is no more guilt. You, my Lord, have saved me from the continued suffering of a tormented mind, body, soul, and spirit. Now I have no more condemnation, for I am in Christ Jesus.

Without you, I was doomed to a limited view, a life without you. Now I am, filled with trust and assurance as I rely on you. Velvet peace covers the senses of my once troubled mind, which was lost, lonely, tormented, and despairing as I looked at each mountain I would have to climb alone.

Now with joy I sing, "No more, no more lost and alone, for you alone, Lord, freed us. As your outstretched hand protects us, 'the Holy Spirit leads and guides us, up every slope in are way straightening and righting the path we should go. My promised companions and mentors in my life are forever the Father, Son, and Holy Spirit. They never allow troubled thoughts to overtake me for long as they guide me along. Now, with each trial, testing, and tribulation, I mature, as you work all things out for my good. I am now content in the comfort of your arms."

I Am Yeshuwa Ha Mashiah

Jesus, the groom, says:

I hear you my love; I hear you my bride.

I embrace you with my love; my arms surround you; my arms protect you.

I present you with my staff of love. I present it to you, my bride, and my soon to be beloved queen.

I kiss your lips with hyssop; I anoint your hands with my love.

I ready you, my bride, and my queen, to present you to the Father, to present you to the Father, for I will give him unto you, and I will give you unto him.

You will be spotless and without wrinkle to glorify him.

My love, my bride, I adore you, my bride, my queen. I have come as your Redeemer. I come as your King.

I am Yeshuwa Ha Mashiah. Just trust in me, my love.

For I have come to give you everlasting life and to impregnate you with my love, with my love.

Comments

So that I could better understand what the Lord was speaking to me through this writing, I looked up some key words in a Bible concordance and Webster's dictionary. *Staff* means, "A stick or rod used for support, a weapon, a symbol of authority, shepherd's protection" (Ps. 23:4).

Impregnate means "to make pregnant, fertilize, to saturate, and to imbue with ideas."

Hyssop means, "A fragrant, blue-flowered plant related to the mint."

As I understand it, *Yeshuwa Ha Mashiah* means "Jesus the Messiah."

I believe I was inspired by the Holy Spirit to write this many years before I had the vision of the "The staff of love." The drawing of the staff is in this book. It is all a matter of faith.

Promise Fulfilled

The bride of Christ says:

E. C.

My eyes 'are focused looking straight ahead, transfixed by the Lord's magnificent image, a point at which the light of his love and compassion emanate from him.

Like a magnet, my Lord draws me. The world no longer has a hold on me, for he has become my delight and desire. Thus, he gives us great hope, for he has promised to give us our heart's desires if we delight in him (Ps. 37:4).

My vision is fixed' on him, for I see him with spiritual eyes, focused on the promise of his second coming. For at the last trump, the dead in Christ shall rise. We are they who see, know, and love him; they will become like him in the twinkling of an eye. No longer will they perish for lack of a vision, for he has promised that whosoever believeth in him should not perish but have eternal life (Prov. 29:18; John 3:16).

I am, securely fastened to him, for he has become my center. I am a new creature, walking in the Spirit, not fulfilling the lust of the flesh. I am going from glory to glory as the Holy Spirit leads me. For now, we see through a glass darkly, but then face-to-face; now I know in part, but then shall I know even as I am, known. "Now abide faith, hope, and love, these three; but the greatest of these is love." (1Cor. 13:12–13)

Focus is "a point at which rays, as of light or sound, meet or diverge or appear to diverge, especially the point at which an image is formed by mirror, lens, or optical system; adjustment, as of eyes or eyeglasses that gives clear vision; central point, center."

As the Comforter, the Holy Spirit leads and guides me through this dark world to see the truth of it. I hear the Lord softly saying to me, "I did go to prepare a place for you, my beloved; for eyes have not seen nor ears heard what I have prepared for those that love me." His pure Word does he speak to me. I am rejoicing, no longer bound by earthly desires, for he has set me free, little by little, precept upon precept, from the pull of earth's gravity.

The things of this world no longer have a hold on me, for I am no longer of this world. I am part of it but not of it, for the truth has set me free.

The bride-church 'was promised, by the Father to his Son Jesus Christ.

As I struggle to stand on terra firma, my eyes see this vision of the Father holding up his Son for the entire world to see: Jesus, the Light of the World, the light of the Father's glorious Son. This penetrating power goes into the deep recesses of the world, expelling the darkness everywhere.

With outstretched hands, Jesus the groom beckons. "Come, all you who love me. My bride, you are beautiful and as a terrible as an army with banners, for there is a set time for you to rule and reign with me for a thousand years (Songs 6:4).

Octave of Love

Bride: "In my frustration and lack of understanding, I cried, 'What more can I do, for I have forsaken all to follow you, my Lord? How much higher can I pitch?'"

Groom: "I would say to you, 'be at peace, for I am with you to help you, to ascend to the eighth octave (a musical interval embracing eight degrees) that I sing in, my beloved bride.'"

Bride: "My Lord, I thought this was a time of rest, a place of *pianissimo* ("very softly"). Now you are calling me up to a *crescendo* ("increasing in loudness") to scale higher. Once again, I surrender to your embrace the eighth octave (musical embrace) of your will, my King."

Groom: "Trust me to complete the good work I have begun in you, for I am the master conductor. I will take you to a *crescendo* (increasing in loudness), and you will come to a place of total surrender, taking your directions only from me. Total rapture is where I will bring you. *Presto*, suddenly will this be. My beloved, you have yet to experience the *crescendo* of my will for your life in me. "Take heart, my love, as my love transforms you from death into resurrected life. You will no longer sing alone, for I am increasing the tempo of my love, creating mercy, great grace, and favor with God and man. *'Allegro, allegro'* (a brisk, lively tempo) beloved of mine' *allegro*. Keep the tempo of faith."

Bathing Light

Bride: "The flowing, flowering petals like a *flower* of our love freely falling onto sacred ground. As a hush fills the earth, it vibrates like ultrasound waves that have penetrated the recesses of the earth, and our hearts, for it is two-dimensional, a trembling of love is sweet utterance. Tender moments of compassion overwhelm me with your tender mercy. I surrender to your love's embrace as an iridescent, luminescent, silver light bathes me, infusing me with renewed life and hope that emanates from you, my King, for 'you are the source of all life. "This bathing light radiates from above, a luminescent and reflective light as it covers us, for we are the object of the Father's great love, his favor and tender mercy flowing, arising in our hearts. This moment in time 'cannot be erased. With renewed hope in our hearts, we rebound, springing back into a renewed life in anticipation of your return, for we have drawn from living waters, the source of all life."

Groom: "My love, we are forever bound to holy ground, for I AM that I AM your surety, my beloved bride. This is just a foretaste of what is yet to come."

Bride: "My beloved King, you are clothed with living light that will bring resurrection life to us. Your beauty is timeless and wonderfully enthroned in the Father's majestic grace, for it is your beauty that emanates tranquil peace. You are the Prince of Peace and not of this turbulent world. For the promise of your return marks the world by your Holy Spirit, renewing hope. It is inexplicable 'revive us, my beloved, revive us. "Renew us like raindrops caught in midair, breathing and creating new life in parched ground after the rain, like dewdrops shimmering in the sun, renewing new hope of your return. Your piercing eyes see through my very soul, causing me to cry, 'Lord, if you see any wicked way in me, take it from me, for your blood covers me.'

E. C.

"For I have tasted your lips of pure honey, your words, and now my heart longs only for you. In rhythm with your tender mercies, I thrill at your nearness. It takes my breath away—like death—yet I live to become more like you. Yet in truth, as I die, I will live for eternity with you."

Comment

A *flower* is "a plant cultivated for its blossoms or the best part: for example, the finest part of a vigorous period, a state of blooming or flourishing." We are cultivated, refined, and improved on by the Holy Spirit tilling the field of our hearts, leading and guiding us into the truth. Is this not wonderful, church, to be blossoming flourishing in his likeness and image? One day we will be just like him.

Cloistered in My Arms

Groom: "My, bride has been maligned, abused, and falsely accused and has suffered from the doctrines of men who have usurped my Word, twisting it for their gain, holding by force, without right, my beloved. Now my Holy Spirit is coming forth to break all that binds her, for my blood covers her. I have set her apart for a season to heal her heart—a broken vessel was she—but I have remolded and reshaped her to fill her with my grace, mercy, compassion for humanity and with the power of my love for humanity.

"I am setting her free to praise and worship me, for no other gods will there be before her.

"I am forevermore my beloveds, and she is mine. No harm will come near her dwelling, for she is my dwelling place. Now, take heart, for the Enemy has tried to sift her as wheat, and he has failed. You see, when my beloved accepted me as her Savior, a covenant 'was made. Now I will never leave or forsake her. For my life's light is within her to shine forth in and through her. Fear not, my love, lasting harm will never, never overtake you, for I am with you.

"I AM that I AM, and I will blot out Amalek from among you. I will not spare Agag as Saul did. The love of money is the root of all evil, and like Saul, these false ones proclaim, 'Blessed be the Lord' and claim that they alone have performed the commandment of the Lord. They have huddled together to lie and to hide the wealth that I said to destroy from among them. I will once again make a show of the Enemy openly. Now, to all of you who have forsaken all to follow me: I will supply all that you need if you trust me, never boasting or praising yourself because of the blessings that will come forth...ready to disperse them at my direction.

"Now, in order for my blessings to flow forth, you must stay humble before me. I come to set my church free from the false doctrines of men, for it is time for my end-time harvest. Now, make ready and prepare yourself.

"*Seed-faith* is a misnomer. I am Jesus, and I am the only good seed to plant in the hearts of men. The Holy Spirit fertilizes and tills the good soil of your heart. I am the only way, and any other-way seed planted in your heart will not produce a harvest of souls. Any other seed you plant will perish and pass away, but my Word shall never pass away. I came to set men free, not to make them wealthy—not as the world knows wealth and prosperity—for again I say the love of money is the root of 'all-evil. I fulfill your need, not your greed.

"As you trust in me and put my kingdom and my righteousness first, then all these other things shall be added unto you. I will pour out blessings you cannot contain, as you trust in me alone, for I own the cattle on a thousand hills and so much more than you can ever imagine. If you knew the Father's heart, you would see that wealth and the treasures of this world are, and will always be, the children—the lost, hurting, and dying of this world (Matt 6:19–34). For I came to 'give them life, and that more abundantly. Not as the world gives, give I unto you. Take note if you have accumulated wealth, riches, and power in this world. You will wrestle with it greatly to stay humble before the Father."

Comments

A *misnomer* is a wrong or inappropriate name or designation.

Please read all the chapters of the epistle of James in the King James Version.

Chapter 4
The Lord's Staff of Love

The Dream of Staff

I had this dream in 2008. In this dream, I saw a beautiful staff, and I heard a voice say, "This staff was fashioned by the Master's own hands, carved from the wooden cross that was sprinkled with his blood. He fashioned this staff with great care, cutting and shaping it to be a precision instrument for his beloved's use. It will produce music and songs for him.

"She will have his authority to do his will on earth as it is in heaven, drafting for him in many ways with shapes and forms. I will present to her my staff of love, for she is under my protection. My beloved wife will have my *divine nature* and *authority*, my DNA, because my blood has cleansed and purified her. Behold, old things have passed away, and behold all things have become new."

What I saw and heard was beyond me. I drew and wrote what I had seen and heard, as best as I could. I asked searched Scripture to verify and confirm my dream (Isa. 64:4: 1 Cor. 15:51–58; Rev. 19:6–10; 2 Cor. 5:17), for his beloved will rule and reign with him in this world and the next, to glorify him (Rom. 8:1–39).

Christ's Reflection

Holy Spirit, birth forth Christ in me, pushing out all that is not of him in me. Let it be according to your Word by faith this very day. In this transformation the world will see the beauty of his holiness, Christ's reflection in you and me, his beloved church. For John the Baptist said that he that hath the bride (church) is the bridegroom, but the friend of the bridegroom (John the Baptist) stands and hears him, rejoicing greatly because of the bridegroom's voice. In this his joy was satisfied, for Christ must increase but John the Baptist must decrease (John 3:29–30).

This is what we must desire also, dear church: that Christ would increase and we would decrease. Knowing Christ and walking with him brings joy forever and a proclamation like Paul's: "It is no longer I that live but Christ." Holy Spirit, please bring forth his majesty in me, for he chose me from among the many 'that were called. I was lost in the darkness when I heard him call to me, and as I drew closer to him, he drew close to me, dispelling the darkness in and around me.

Now I cannot live without him. No longer, am I satisfied with half measures; I desire the fullness of him. Oh Holy Spirit, oh Holy Spirit, help me. For it is written' let it be according to my faith, for faith comes by hearing and hearing by the word of God, and Jesus is the Word. I hear him so clearly now, because I sit at his feet. Once I sought him in the *broad way* and found him not there. Then the Holy Spirit reminded me that the broad way leads to destruction, and there are many who go there and eat. Straight is the gate and narrow is the way that leads unto life, and few there be that find it (Songs 3:2; Matt. 7:13).

In that moment I took hold of the impossible; I believed the improbable, that he would choose a common field flower like me—a rose of Sharon and a lily of the valley.

Then I heard him say, "Yes, my beloved, a lily that grows among the roses' thorns, one so lost and full of sin, of little worth or value to anyone but me, one who stumbled at every turn." Then he continued, "I wept. By the Father's grace and mercy, my dove, you stopped long enough to hear me say, "I love you just the way you are, darkened by the earth's (glitter) sun. Believe in me, for I am your Savior, your betrothed. Yield to the Holy Spirit who guards you, and he will lead and guide you to me, teaching you to learn of me, my beloved one.

"Believe in the power of my blood to cleanse and purify you for my use, making you white as newly fallen snow. For 'thou art all fair, my love. There is no spot in thee because of me."

I have come a long way it has been a journey of faith, a rocky road made smooth, for he went before me to prepare the way down the path he traversed before me, thus making 'my way sure.

A surer way he could not make to bless us, for he left no stone unturned, making himself our sure foundation and thus preparing his promise that one day he would come back for us and we would be just like him in all of his glory. Reflecting his beautiful likeness and image of purity in body, mind, soul, and spirit, we will be whole and holy undefiled before God and man. For he died for you and me, purifying us with his holy shed blood, and now we are destined to stand in his righteous presence, free from all guilt or wrong, free to be his queen, his crowning glory for eternity.

Cherish His Love

Joy comes from embracing the cross of Christ Jesus, thus freeing the Holy Spirit to lead and guide us into the truth. We come just as we are, unrefined in our fallen state, for old habits are hard to break. We pick up our cross daily and follow Jesus, studying to make ourselves approved as workers of God.

A peace that passes all understanding will envelop us; a joy unspeakable to behold and full of his glory encircles us in the everlasting knowledge that he will complete the good work he has begun in us. This truth gives us the hope to hold dear the "blessings of the cross," treating them with care.

Rejoicing, we cherish the promise of his second return, for he said he would never leave us or forsake us. Beloved church, our Lord Jesus Christ will return with a shout to do what he has promised he will do. Now, look up, for our redeemer and redemption draws nigh, for he is not a man that he should lie.

Consoled by His Comfort

As I entered into your presence, the winds of adversity fell to the ground, for even the winds ceased at your command. As you extended your hand of comfort to me, you reached into the very depths of my heart, making it pliable and yielded to your will. The Great Physician gently massaged new life back into my stony, broken heart.

I was consoled. By his life-giving blood, by his love, he freed me from a life drenched with sin. I was one of the lost hurting, and dying of this world—so alone, so very alone, never full, always empty. I 'was misshapen by a life 'full of sin and surrounded by the consequences of that sin, unable to understand the misery I felt! I never fit in nor 'was I accepted until I realized my destiny was always to be with Jesus and not of this world.

A stony heart had I, made this way by life's circumstances. I was lost and alone, even in a crowded room. I was never full, always empty as I 'was led astray by ones I trusted. I was young and confused, and I had no voice of my own. I was silent and without protest. I was a fighter with no fight left inside of me. I became an unwilling vessel for abuse by those who claimed to love me.

Then, as I accepted my beloved Lord Jesus Christ, he comforted me, filling me with his love. Now my cup overflows with joy that is unspeakable to behold and full of his glory. As he continually and tenderly massaged my stony heart and made it one of flesh, a new life of faith and hope surged through me, extinguishing my pain, anger, and resentment, and the pride of life began to fade. The infilling of the Holy Spirit and the fire of his love rules my life now and readies me for a banqueting table that awaits his beloved bride.

Those who love him will traverse the heavens, the universe with him—no longer tethered to this world and grasping for pure air, free from sin, our minds renewed. For our lives will be in harmony with him, transformed by God's grace and mercy and his Son's life-giving blood his selfless love. We are now destined to bask in the comfort of that love (1 Cor. 14:33; Matt. 8:26–27; Ezek. 11:19; Songs 2:2–4; Rev. 19:9).

His Reward Is with Him

(Matt. 25:1–13; Rev. 22:12)

Then shall, the kingdom of heaven, 'be likened unto ten virgins that took their lamps and went forth to meet the bridegroom. Moreover, five of them were wise and five were foolish. They that were foolish took their lamps and took no oil with them, but the wise took oil in their vessels with their lamps full.

"I am the Good Shepherd," Jesus said. "Verily, verily I say unto you, he that enters not by the door into the sheepfold [shelter for the sheep] but climbs up some other way, he is a thief and a robber. However, he that enters in by the door is the shepherd of the sheep" (John 10:1–2). Jesus is the only way, truth, and life. He is the door. However, many foolish people have not yielded to the Holy Spirit and prepared themselves for his return. Nevertheless, a few wise people will.

Jesus is the only way, truth, and life, and no one comes to him unless the Father draws them for he does not waste his time on the foolish. Jesus' beloved, his wise ones, hear his voice, and another they will not follow. She was and filled with the anointing of the Holy Spirit through the washing of the water of the Word, trusting not in another to keep her full of the oil from the Word. This beloved vessel is like an oil lamp with a *wick* trimmed to burn a flame that produces light and heat.

She is a bundle of soft fibers that draw up the Holy Spirit's anointing, a *wick* that has been ignited and trimmed, cutting her *wick* of "self-will" daily, thus defeating the enemy resoundingly. This she does with the consuming fire of God's love, for she is the lover of his soul. She has become one with him and is now prepared to set the captives free. Pure, holy, and undefiled for she recognized her Messiah as one greater than Solomon. Who is now in the midst of her! She comes to glorify her Lord, putting on her Lord's mantle for eternity. She becomes like unto a lacy sheath, and he enfolds and envelops her as she draws closer, closer to him. She becomes incandescent, for she has placed her will over the consuming fire of his love. Her, *Wick a loosely bound bundle of soft fibers that draws up oil*

A twofold ministry do I give to thee; you have, been 'set apart for my purpose, for my kingdom knows no barriers. Now, behold I come quickly; and my reward is with me, to give every man according as his work. Therefore, shall it be (Rev. 22:1–21).

Chapter 5
Shofar

    I referenced page 405 of *The Power New Testament* by William J. Morford, which explains what a shofar is. One Greek word 'was used to translate both *shofar* and *trumpet*. The shofar 'was used to call to repentance, and many think that the feast referred to as the Day of Memorial in Leviticus 23:24 will be Judgment Day, which is also a call to repentance. We call this the Feast of Trumpets, but the Hebrew Scriptures include neither the feast nor trumpet.

E. C.

The shofar is the instrument used (1 Cor. 15:52; 1 Thess. 4:16 *The Power New Testament*).

The Trumpet is also a symbol of prophetic utterance.

Clarion Call

I was still, waiting for my beloved's return, with my spiritual ears attuned to every movement and sound, trying every spirit to see if it was of God. In this stillness, I suddenly heard a rustling that filled the trees and penetrated through the branches and down the vines, inflaming my senses. Then, in the hush that ensued, I heard a voice.

This sure, pure sound filtered down from the trees to me as if suspended in midair. Then your voice caressed the tips of the olive leaves, making them quiver, so brilliantly clear was your voice. Then you said that only a few would hear it, for many had been called yet few will chose to obey the call, for their spirits were willing but the flesh was weak.

The voice of Jesus is so strong yet gentle. When I heard his call, the pitch of his voice was beyond perfection, his voice vibrating in perfect tones from every instrument— and some I had never heard before—for his voice was in monotones of a perfect pitch and level not of this world.

As I was immersed in the perfect sounds of him—in the sound of this music' I had never heard before yet the tone was familiar to me—the experience seemed to be a paradox. Instinctively I knew it' was a new song, one I had never heard, but it was a song I seemed to know. How could this be? Then, with great compassion in his voice, I heard him say, "This song was in my heart, composed for you before from the foundation of the world: for God so loved the world that he gave his only begotten Son, and I have known you, my beloved, from before the foundations of the world.

His clarion voice continued to resonate in my heart with this dialogue:

Groom: "I have loved you, and I will love you time without end. From Genesis to Revelation have I done this for you, for I love you beyond measure. This is my song of remembrance to remind you that I shed my blood for you. It is a song of salvation and eternal life and is the promise of the healing of the nations."

Bride: "As I cupped my hands over my face, I wept. Then he said, 'my beloved, do not cry. Rejoice and sing this new song with me, telling the whole world 'all about the Father's true prosperity, for it is not of this world. My only begotten Son is the world's prosperity, and my prosperity will never pass away but will give you everlasting life. Heaven and earth shall pass away, but my word shall never pass away'" (Matt. 24:35).

Groom: "Ask them if the kingdoms of this world can offer them more. For the world's prosperity is fleeting at best. I make old things pass away, and behold, all things have become new. Oh, ye of little faith, can the world do this for you?"

Bride: "This is my beloved's song of love, and it will revive us, for the truth sets us free. It is a beautiful clarion call, like a misting breeze suspended in midair, obscuring my beloved from view. It has refreshed my very soul. It is our

Lord and King calling to us to make ready. For a season, you 'have been hidden in him, waiting for his voice to call you to come forth from confinement. He is clearly calling us to make ready, beloved ones, for we 'have been trained, tried, tested, and found true it is up to you. It is time for battle! "For our weapons are not carnal but mighty through God, to the pulling down of strongholds. He has filled you with gifts and callings without measure. This is a song for the redeemed, a call to come out of all that has been perverted and twisted in his Word and this world. For my Lord makes a sure sound, not one that scatters the flock and a stranger will not follow Him. It is a call to repent and refresh in his love. "It is a call to war, for the harvest is plenty but the laborers are few. It is a call to pull down every stronghold of the enemy in his beloved church. His soon-to-be-crowned queen she will rule and reign with him for eternity."

Groom: "A double whirlwind of despair comes with the enemy's prosperity, for you reap what you sow and where your treasure is, that is where your heart will be also. The world is in turmoil, shaken to its very core by sin; there foundations—natural and spiritual—are crumbling. It is not by my Hand of judgment but your own destruction comes upon you for you call "good evil and evil good" cursing what God has blessed. America has lost her footing, for I AM is no longer her sure foundation. I AM that I AM calling you to come back, come back to me, for I am your Creator, the Savior of the world. Come unto me, all you who are heavy-laden, and I will give you rest for your souls."

Bride: "Then I suddenly heard a rushing, mighty wind through the trees. Fire exploded, igniting God's love, and the Holy Spirit—the Holy Spirit was everywhere. Revival took place in the air, doing violence to the Prince of the Air. A man-made vortex has destroyed and done great harm to America and the world, and if it is not stopped, it will continue."

Groom: "Ready yourself. If you heed my call, I will position you in my end-time army. So-called "prosperity" preachers, teachers, and prophets will continue to be an obstacle. They do not qualify, for they feed the flesh and not the spirit. These are some of the ones that 'will be left behind for another chance to repent. Moreover, some are too stubborn and arrogant, and they refuse to change. However, I am not willing that any man should perish, and some of them will go through their own destruction much tribulation."

Comments

Please note the date this text 'was written was in 2010 as I was checking my edited text of "Clarion Call" the date today is 11/5/2012 I was reminded of the terrible storm that just hit New York and surrounding areas and neighboring states! 'Tomorrow we elect a new president of America, and the Holy Spirit told me a while back, while in prayer even before I knew who the republican candidate would be! That I have sent you a man after my own heart and if those who 'are called by my name come out in force to vote him in office good change will accrue if not much confusion and destruction will continue of a magnitude not seen take place yet! Therefore, we will see church that it was never in the Lords hands but ours. Also for a long time I have heard the word *vortex, vortex* in my mind and I wrote a message about it that is not in

E. C.

this book but it did say in simple words that it would be a *vortex of blessings,* or a *vortex of turmoil* and *destruction.* I understand why now...Some prayed for a *Saul* and I sent them a *Saul* but with Saul, I have sent you *David* and a way of escape but you refuse to put your differences aside and my blessing has passed you by, you continue to call evil good and good evil. By your own hand and stubborn ways, you have shortened your days for there is a set time for revival. For I come quickly.

How, often do I have to send this word to you, before you head my warning, you stubborn generation!

"If my people who are called by my name shall humble there self and pray and seek my face,

And turn from there wicked ways; then will I hear from heaven, and will forgive there sin and

I will heal there land."(II Chr. 7: 14) Lord I humbly pray for the awaking of the Church please

Lord! "Blow ye the trumpet in Zion, and sound the alarm in my holy mountain: for the day of

The, Lord cometh, for it is nigh at hand. Joel 2:1, 8" Lord please forgive are wicked ways and

Call, us to repent!

Comments

[These are my original comments for this text "Clarion Call"]

Over, and over, as the heavens 'were filled with strange weather and unusual tornadoes, I heard the word *vortex.* From 2008 to 2012, I kept hearing the words 'man-made tornadoes.

Revival is now in the air, for God goes before us to prepare the way (2 Cor. 10:4). Revival can only come after death—in this case, death to our self-will. We must hear the trumpeting of the Lord for he is calling the bride to battle to rescue the children the lost hurting and dyeing of this world!

Please understand I do not consider myself a prophet just, a woman of prayer.

The word *clarion* means "brilliantly clear."

The word *vortex* means "something resembling a whirlpool-tornado"

Please understand that when God picks someone he looks at the *heart*, not what affiliation (church) thy grew up with, or is in, or if thy even know him yet. For he has chosen us from the foundations of the world thank goodness for he did not give up on me, but he knew me, before I knew him. The only test I go by now is the test Jesus left us-you shall know my disciples by the Love they have for one another. STOP blocking the way of the lost! For at one time I was lost' but thanks to the drawing of the Holy Spirit he saw my heart, drew me to the truth, and set me free. DO NOT PLAY INTERFEARANCE WITH THE HOLY SPIRIT FOR YOU WILL LOSE-for one of the promises of God is that the Holy Spirit will lead and guide us and show us all things even the hidden things (of the heart) that men try to hide.

The Lord speaks repeatedly to you-I have sent different denominations to you, and you just ridicule, embarrass them, and shake your bible in the air at them, instead of embracing them with my words of compassion and love gently entreating them. In addition, you profess to know whom David was, what nonsense with all your head knowledge you do not even know me, like the Sadducees and Pharisees of my day. Warning- I Chr. 16:22 this is most interesting that the Holy Spirit would use this verse for it is written by David as part of a psalm of thanksgiving. You think you know David, he was flawed but always thankful no matter what' and he praised his wonderful working God. How foolish man is, to try to manipulate to <u>do</u> and hide things behind the Lords back. The Lord said to me a long time ago when I did not think I could endure anymore, pray for your enemy's Evelyn for I will defend you with an out stretched arm and a fist of iron and I will thwart the enemy's plans for your sake and he continues to do so. Maybe one day if the Lord tarries, I will wright about his marvelous intervention on my behalf. Many years ago a preacher encouraged me with these words-Young lady you have a big vision hold on to it and see what God will do with it' and I am. My vision is this if he can save me he can save anyone except those who (blatantly, lie) blasphemy against the Holy Spirit. Rev. 3: 14—22; Mark 3:28—30

Prince of Peace Speaks into 2013

Hear oh my people 'who are called by my name, you, who are living and holding fast to the past injustices and what it did to you and your ancestors, who were sold into slavery as your <u>Jewish brothers</u> were, and forced to become *servants to all!* You who refuse to *forgive* *"till seven times"* are withholding my blessings, glory, gifts from yourself and the blessings of my kingdom and my will be done in you and your children's life, ignoring my word which is "If you want to be the greatest in the kingdom of God be a *servant to all."* Your faith in my word <u>allows</u> me to turn bad into good for you, for without faith it is impossible to please God. Matt. 5: 44, 18:1—35 Peace beloved ones read Eph. 1: 1—23, 2: 1—22

My beloved I now place this into your *hands* for save keeping and leave it there for you to *contemplate* on this New Year of *tribulations*, to test and fulfill if you will, or not. For all that he asks you to do for his kingdom sake, is nothing he has not done for us and much more, for he went before us. Some *false* leaders have led you *astray*, for there is no <u>*forgiveness*</u> in them. For they continue to *curse* what God has *blessed* and bring judgment down on your homes and the house of God and <u>*America*</u> because they agree with the enemy. For you do not study my word on your own, depending sole on trusting the guidance of the Holy Spirit, thus you are unable to try every *spirit* with a humble and contrite spirit and a forgiving heart. Rom. 12: 14, Gal. 6: 7—10

Hypocrites' Matt. 23: 1—39 these are they who are 'greedy for gain that flees the flock for their prosperity and will lose their very soul, do not tolerate them. I believe this year of two thousand and thirteen will begin the battle against rebellion, backsliding, apostasy in the church through the blessed <u>*unity*</u> of the Holy Spirit. Eps.4: 1—32, 5:1—33, 6: 1—18

I'AM that I' AM the *Prince of Peace* and only I can bring *peace* to Israel, you and the hurting world, what is it that you desire of me, that I have not already done and given to you? Place the *mantle* of my *grace* and <u>*love*</u> around you, walk by <u>*faith*</u> beside me..., and cry aloud the Spirit and the bride say come! Humble your-self under the mighty hand of God <u>*repent*</u> and you will see <u>*revival*</u> in the land in the mist of all the turmoil you <u>*elected*</u> to have, for beloved I come quickly.

The *hope* is in us church, for greater is he who is in me-us, then he who is in the world. <u>*Believe*</u> beloved <u>*Believe*</u> for we are more than conquers through Christ Jesus. Do not just roll over and play dead, fight the good fight of faith never go by what you see hear and feel and take a stand for what you believe in, for faith-love without works is dead. Love one another, love one another as I love you, forgive one another as I have forgiven you, says the Lord of hosts' never, never give up on your love ones, placing them in our Lords hands is our faith in action, for he will complete the good work he has begun in them, also. When we place our grain of mustard seed faith in the Father, Sons-blood sacrifice, and the working of the Holy Spirit, then are faith will move mountains, and cast our mountains into the sea, we must shake off the old and hold fast to the new. For some in ministry you have loved, will not, through away all their false words and fellow the Lords teaching, because of their false pride. When he warns you to leave, never look back!

Beloved covet to prophesy, now check what you are prophesying in to the world. Let us prophesy love, joy, peace and a sound mind, joy unspeakable to be hold and full of his glory! That everything that is bad that I see, hear or feel this New Year I will rejoice over because my **_Good God_** turns bad into good for you and me that all things will work together for *good* to them who love the Lord. Let us be determined not to let evil overcome *good*, but to overcome evil with *good*. For as long as we are in the flesh we cannot block all evil out, so pray and bind it, for if we go by what we see hear and feel we will be defeated and deflated, for the Enemy of our souls is pure evil.

However, the Lord Jesus is the lover of our souls and he is pure and holy Yes, beloved ones sing praises to our soon coming King and let everything that has breath praise our Lord Jesus Christ for nothing is too hard for him. *Believe*, beloved *Believe*, for there is much tribulation ahead, for time is very, very short the Enemy is furious and knows his time is short for he has deluded himself into thinking this time would never come.

E.C. 12/8/2012

Note: Once again, I believe the Hebrew interpretation for the word widow means-a woman without a voice. When I heard this, I became very sad because I was a widow. However, the Holy Spirit comforted me with these words "you now have the Lords voice for you are betroth to Him." Yes, beloved sing we 'are betrothed to Him.

Chapter 6
Pearl Drops of Wisdom

(Proverbs 8:1–36; 9:10)

Jesus instructed us to turn the other cheek, but he never said we had to like it. Surely, we, his church, do not have to stick around for more, duck, and cover church! We are troops for our commander-in-chief, Jesus Christ, and he always makes a way of escape. Put on the full armor of God.

Always stay on defense, with the blood of the Lamb and the word of our testimony for the Enemy goes about seeking whom he might devour. He the Enemy is on offence he attacks and assaults our senses. We must try every spirit to see if it is of God. We must resist the Devil, and he will flee from us. Henceforth we are no more children, tossed back and forth and carried about by every wind of doctrine or by the sleight of cunning and crafty men who lie in wait to deceive us. Satan's false disciples use the Word of God to confuse us. The kingdoms of this world and their power and glory tempt us. In the same way Jesus was tempted, so are we...we must know the truth as Jesus did.

As a predator, Satan comes to steal, kill, and destroy us with his polluted and perverted version of the gospel. Satan will never change; he is the same yesterday, today, and forever, for he imitates and is the opposite of God. If our minds 'are not renewed with the washing of the water of the Word, then we are destroyed every day for our lack of knowledge of the pure Word of God. Jesus said it was better that he left earth, for he would send the Comforter, the Holy Spirit, to lead and guide us into the truth.

Grab hold of the Holy Spirit and do not let go, for he will lead you through to the other side safely.

Jesus said, "Get thee behind me, Satan; for it is written, Thou shalt worship the Lord thy God and him only shalt thou serve." (Matt.4: 10)

We must speak the truth, in and out of season, for the truth sets us free to be about the Father's business as our Lord Jesus did. Resist the Devil, and he will flee with his tail between his legs. "Defeating the Enemy with the words of Jesus in Matt.4:4, 7, 10"

If there is anything in 'this book that is not of the Lord Jesus Christ, I pray that it be cast away from you, for my intent is to bless and encourage his beloved church.

Chapter 7
His Bride's Attributes

(Matthew 5:1–12)

His beloved is humbled in order to become poor in spirit. By God's grace, she is humbled under his mighty hand that she might acknowledge her sinful nature and her total dependence upon the cross of Jesus Christ to save her. Now, theirs is the kingdom of heaven (Ps. 1:1–6; Matt. 26:1–13).

His beloved will mourn, for she will experience much grief and sorrow, finding little comfort or mercy in this world. Her dependence on man and the things of this world will decrease, thus increasing her dependence on her Lord Jesus Christ and the Holy Spirit, for her only true comfort comes as the Comforter leads and guides her into the truth.

By learning to obey through her suffering, his beloved becomes meek, patiently enduring injury without resentment. By giving her burdens to her Lord Jesus Christ, she becomes more and more like him, picking up her cross daily to follow him. For the Lord, who is meek and lowly, is calling us who are heavy-laden to come unto him, and he will give us rest as we sit at his feet and learn of him.

His beloved hungers and thirsts after righteousness in order to understand the meaning of being truly free from guilt or wrong, in order to stand upright before God the Father. She has a strong desire for the truth, an urgent need for the bread of life. Because of this longing for the truth, she shall be filled until her cup overflows.

His beloved is merciful, because she obtained mercy by God's grace and compassion. The blessings arrived through his divine favor, which was, freely given by the shedding of his Son's blood on the cross, for Jesus paid the ultimate price for the remission of sins for all those who believe in him. They are now in harmony with one another, in one accord.

In reaping mercy from her Lord Jesus, she can now *sow* mercy into others' lives. In this, she shows God's love for them, thus scattering abroad in their hearts his mercy toward them.

His beloved is pure in heart, for the fire of God's love has tried the reins of her heart, purifying her for her Lord's use. Now she shall see God.

His beloved is a peacemaker, for the reflected light in her proclaims the gospel of peace. Because of this, she shall do greater works. Multitudes 'shall be saved, and they too will be called the children of God, for she has this promise: that she shall do greater works for the Father.

His bride is 'persecuted for righteousness' sake in order to open up her understanding to what is just and honorable, that she might be free from guilt. Becoming upright before her Lord, She will not suffer the children to come unto him: for theirs is the kingdom of heaven (1 Pet. 3:14).

His bride is reviled and persecuted, and all manner of evil and spoken against her falsely for her Lord's sake. Now hers is the kingdom of heaven.

His bride is blessed and rejoices and is exceedingly glad when men revile her and persecute her, for great is her reward in heaven. For so persecuted they the prophets that were before her (Eph. 4:13; Rev. 22:1–21).

His beloved's character change only comes forth when she has chosen to follow Jesus and not man, thus drawing her even closer to her Lord Jesus Christ after every trial, tribulation, and testing of faith that comes her way. She endures it all, because he has never left her side, even when she took a wrong turn or stumbled on the way. He just picked her up, dusted her off, and gently led her down the right path that led to him.

How do I know all of this? Because the Good Shepherd, our Lord Jesus Christ, took his "staff of love" and lifted me out of the ditch of miry clay I had fallen in. For, I was a baby in Christ Jesus' and burdened down by habitual sins and the cares of this world. Yet by his grace I learned to lean on him and hear his voice and no other. This is my story and song, for he freed me from the law of sin and death and replaced my hard heart with a new melody of His sweet love, reviving and renewing my hard heart, now my heart desire is for him.

For his beloved now sees her calling and understands that not many who are wise after the flesh, not 'many mighty and not many noble are called. For God has chosen the foolish things of the world to confound the wise; and God has chosen the weak things of the world to confound the things that are mighty; and the base things that are despised has God chosen; yes, and things that are not he uses to bring to nothing things that are. This is so that no flesh should glory in his presence (1 Cor. 1:25–31).

As a newborn baby in Christ, I heard false teachers preach and false prophets prophesy. They were and are everywhere in the church, and they continually lied, fleecing the flock, shearing me of my faith-covering and shelter, confusing me because I was so young in the Lord. Through the things I suffered, I learned to recognize the false ones who gloried in appearances and not in the changing of the heart.

This confused me when it happened, and the Holy Spirit would use what little of the Word was in me at that time to gently pick me up, dust me off, and draw me safely back into his presence to embrace me as I studied his Word. Then, as I drew fresh water to drink (the Word), he would speak to me as he did to the woman at the well, for he knew all that I had done. Then he would tell me to repent and to go on telling others what he had done for me, for his blood covered me.

Then he would comfort me with his Word, saying, "My beloved, I will never leave you or forsake you, for my promises are *yes* and *amen* to all who love me, and you have forsaken all to follow me. For you 'were promised, to me, by my Father. You are my beloved bride, soon to be my beloved queen. Now, drink of me, the living water that is set before you, and I will turn things around for you. Repent as you yield to me, for old, sinful habits are hard to break. Trust me."

As I grew in Christ Jesus, I became more proficient in the knowledge of him. Through much persecution, trial, and tribulation, I trusted and believed in him, not in what I saw, heard, and felt.

I now have a knowing peace that passes all understanding. It is not *I* that live but *he*, for it is not by my power or by my might but by His Holy Spirit, says the Lord. I thank you, blessed 'Holy Spirit, that the Word of God is now in my heart; the Word of God is alive in me. Because of this, I will never stop growing in the knowledge of your only begotten Son, Father God.

Beloved ones do not despair, for he will complete the good work he has begun in us. Believe, for he is not a man that he should lie (Phil. 1:6).

His bride's commission is to lift up Jesus for the entire world to see. He said that if he was lifted up from the earth, he would draw all men to himself. In the natural realm of earth, Jesus died in the flesh. In the spirit realm, these 'are men, who allow the Holy Spirit to "plow under" their flesh (earth/dirt) by the washing of the water of the Word. "But we have this treasure in earthen vessels that the Excellency and the power may be of God and not of us." (II Cor. 4:7)

I will expound on this, lifting up and lifting away, for there is much that 'is hidden in plain sight that will be revealed in this hour. Now, if we will just listen with our spiritual ears, we will hear what the Holy Spirit is saying to the churches. Jesus taught in parables because he used them to veil the truth from those who were not willing to see it.

Those who really desire to know him will not rest until they find out the true meanings of the mysteries of the parables—in his day and now. For instance, Jesus said to his disciples, "If I be lifted up, I will draw all men to me."

We now know the natural meaning: that Jesus had to 'be crucified so that all men could be saved.

Now, hear the spiritual meaning of this parable mystery, if you will. This is what the Holy Spirit revealed to me—and not only to me, I'm sure, as it is so simple: if we—you and I—lift Jesus Christ up, he will draw all men to him. This is all we 'are called to do: to lift Jesus up in our daily lives through the living Word of God in us. Then that Word in us will do the rest. When we become examples of the good news that is working in us, then we can show others the way to the truth.

Some will produce tenfold and some a hundredfold; this is character change in action, which produces fruit according to our proximity to Jesus. When this happens, his light will shine so brightly through us that it will glorify the Father in heaven. The difference in us will stand out in a crowd, and we will make a difference.

Beloved, the truth sets people free, for Jesus paid the ultimate price for you and me. When we put Jesus first, then all these other 'things shall be added unto us. We are his earthen vessels, temples of the Holy Spirit, and we must now reflect Jesus in all of his love, humility, and grace, lifting him up so the entire world sees *him* rather than ourselves. In order for this to happen, we must decrease so that he will increase—as we pick up our crosses daily and follow him.

Thus, we will fulfill his commandment to love one another as he loves us. As we draw close to him, there will be a longing, a desire to know him—and then a deeper and deeper longing to draw closer to him, with a love that passes all understanding flowing in and through us (Ps. 42:1, 7, 11). Deep calls to deep: this is an ongoing process, and it will be up to us how little or how much we reflect Jesus from now until eternity.

As we our changed from glory to glory, our desire for the things of this world will diminish, and our desire for Jesus will become insatiable. Therefore, we study to make ourselves approved workers unto God, yielding our members, not to our selfish self-wills but to righteousness and holiness and to the Holy Spirit and the full promise of him.

Jesus said to his disciples that it was better for him to leave earth, for he would send to them the Holy Spirit, the Comforter, who would lead and guide them into all truth. His truth sets us free. I believe that as we yield to the Holy Spirit he will greatly convict us of sin and will reveal the knowledge and wisdom of God's great grace to forgive one another. This is the wisdom of God's love-forgiveness. The first forgiven was the thief at the cross and then Jesus forgave us, so we are to forgive one another as he has forgiven us. "Father, forgive them for they know not what they do." (Luke. 23: 34) As the Enemy strips us of our clothes, flaying us with stripes on our backs and thorns in are head, piercing are hands, feet, and side. Thy will be the very ones closes to us, we must forgive them praying for our enemy's as Jesus forgave the malefactor, we to must forgive if he repent and then he will see paradise, our Lord always set the example for us there are few who will walk with him and suffer with him. Scripture references are in-Luke chapter twenty-three.

As we walk parallel to Jesus, he will never require us to do something he has not done for us already. He always goes before us to prepare the way. As we experience the knowledge of him and a desire to be more like him, he merges with our hearts and lives, changing us from glory to glory.

To the very end, Jesus was faithful to God and to man. There was a great "lifting away" as Jesus forgave and great fear descended upon them as he forgave his enemies. Then the veil, the partition in the temple, 'was rent in twain, giving us access to the Father through Jesus. This lifting away of sin 'was done so that we would have the power to choose to live in him.

This is true resurrection power. I will expound on this statement. Two malefactors hung beside Jesus, and one railed at him, but the other rebuked the first, saying, "Dost not thou fear God, seeing thou art in the same condemnation? Moreover, we indeed justly; for we receive the due reward of our deeds: but this man hath done nothing amiss." Therefore, he said unto Jesus, "Lord, remember me when thou comets into thy kingdom." In addition, Jesus said unto him, "Verily I say unto thee, today shalt thou be with me in paradise.

Jesus spoke in parables to the very end (Luke 23:39–43). Herein lies the mystery of these Scriptures (Matt. 20:16; 22:1–14). Many 'are called but few are chosen, just like the two malefactors one will believe and the other will not.

He is calling us all to the banqueting table (Matt. 22:1–14).

Jesus' call came first to the Jews and then to the Greeks (Rom. 1:16), and we will either accept or reject his call—at our own peril (Rev. 19:6–21). Jesus was and is humble; he never had a look-at-me mentality, for his vision was to be with his Father again. He always lifted the Father above himself. His ministry 'was not centered on money, or himself, for Jesus was not full of excess. I believe the Father met his every *need*, not *greed*, for my Lord was without sin, and he did everything in moderation.

The Holy Spirit has taught me how to 'prosper and be in good health, in and through the knowledge of our Lord Jesus Christ and the power of his might, not through the knowledge of the things of this world or by my own flesh but by his Spirit; for I live by faith in him and not by sight. (Heb.11:1)

I have learned that my kingdom is not of this world, for I am no longer of this world. I understand that where my heart is, there my treasure will be also. We have a better promise, for we are now joint heirs with Christ Jesus (Gal. 3:22–29). Jesus redeemed us from the law of sin and death, and now we are sons of God if we faint not (Gal. 6:1–10). We are no longer servants but sons, and if sons, then heirs of God through Christ Jesus.

As long as we are under bondage to the things of this world, we children are no different from servants, even though we are lords of all—except for the fact that we are under tutors and governors until the time appointed of the Father. We are the redeemed, adopted sons of God, and because we are sons, God has sent forth the Spirit of his Son into our hearts, crying, "Abba, Father."

We are no more servants but sons, if we walk in the Spirit, not fulfilling the lust of the flesh; and if we are sons, then we are heirs of God through Christ Jesus (Gal. 4:1–8). This is the mystery and revelation of the manifested sons of God (1 Cor. 15:52–58; 1 Pet. 1:19; 2 Pet. 1:19; 2 Cor. 3:18; 1 Cor. 13:12; Rom. 8:1–39). Beloved, 'we will be changed in the twinkling of an eye, for we will see him as he really is. This recognition of the Lord will certify who are the manifested sons of God.

While on this earth, our Lord Jesus Christ denounced the Scribes and Pharisees in Matthew 23:1–39 for their hypocrisy and excesses. His beloved church will do the same, for we are not on the Good Ship Lollypop, as some would have us believe. We are on the Faith Ship, and when the storms of life come up, our faith should be in Jesus Christ, the Son of the living God not in the things of this world. By our faith in Jesus' name, which is above every name, we must speak to the storms in our lives. Peace, be still and know that he is God (Matt. 8:23–27).

Jesus knew that it would be better for us, his disciples, if he went to the Father so that the Holy Spirit would empower us from on high with faith and fire in our hearts for Jesus. When Jesus rebuked the natural storm for the disciples our Lord was in the same boat with them asleep, yet they were fearful, full of doubt and unbelief. Even to the end of Jesus' life, they were still fearful. After the resurrection, Jesus appeared to the women first because of their faith-filled love for him.

We who believe in him 'are covered with his precious blood, filled with the Holy Spirit and promise. What is our excuse for not trusting in him? Is it our lack of faith and love? If this is the case, let us remind one another that faith works by love for our Lord Jesus Christ and comes by hearing and hearing by the Word of God (Rom. 10:1–21). If you are not content in whatever state you find yourself, then you must ask yourself, "What gospel am I listening to?" The gospel of devils does not bring you contentment, for it feeds your flesh and does not quench your thirst (1 Tim. 4:1–2). Do you have to be inflated or pumped-up in order to feel good about yourself? If so, then you do not know who you are in Christ Jesus, for the truth sets us free.

Man lifts up man and the things of this world and then pursues self-gratification. Man wants you to follow humanity and its teachings. The gospel of Jesus Christ brings contentment and peace that passes all understanding; all you have to do is learn of him and lean on him, and he will complete the good work he has begun in you.

I believe we are in the very last days, when history will repeat itself and come full circle, for some of the Gentiles who knew Christ 'will fall away. Then he will stretch forth his hand once again to Israel, for some who are Jews will hold fast to their confession of faith in Jesus because the truth has set them free, and some will perish for their lack of *vision* or faith in the gospel of Jesus Christ.

The definition of *perish* is "to be destroyed or ruined, to cease to exist." The definition of *vision* is "the act or power of seeing; sight."

Paul was educated in Jewish law and so blinded by his own self-righteousness that he hated and persecuted Jesus and his followers. He 'was bent on destroying them and was spiritually blind, and when Jesus appeared to him in the natural world, the resurrection light coming from Jesus rendered Paul physically blind. In simple words, Paul 'was blinded by the light emanating from Jesus, so that Jesus might open Paul's spiritual eyes to see him. Paul was in great darkness, as we all are without him.

The Lord replaced evil with good, and the rest is history. Even after our Lord Jesus' resurrection, he continued to show us the power of forgiveness with the example of Paul. The wisdom of God's love is forgiveness; it will cause revival (resurrection power) to break forth. Then the dead in Christ shall rise (1 Cor. 2:5–16; 3:1–23). Again, we must decrease so that he will increase.

To quote "Amazing Grace," a song we all can relate to, "I once was blind, but now I see."

Resurrection in the Bible refers to Christ's rising from the dead and to the rising of all dead humans before the final judgment. A *revival* involves 'being brought back to consciousness or activity, making or becoming fresh or strong again, or bringing back into use.

Revival is coming, and we will *arise* and *shine*. (Isa. 60: 1) Wake up and get up, church!

For behold, the darkness shall cover the earth, but the Lord shall *arise* upon thee, and the Gentiles shall 'come to thy light, and kings to the brightness of thy rising. (Isa. 60: 2, 3)

Beloved, believe in the author and finisher of our faith, and do not put your trust in the arm of the flesh, which is our own strength. Then you will no longer be reflective of the phrase, "Oh ye of little faith" but rather the phrase 'Well done, my good and faithful *servant*." Jesus came as a *servant* to all before he became our *King,* and so shall we become a *servant* to all doing the same as are Lord for we walk parallel to Jesus, side-by-side, until we come face-to-face with him and *crowned* his *Queen* (Heb. 13:5).

"When I dock my *ship* in the harbor of life's circumstances, *we must examine ourselves,* "Am I harboring unbelief? Am I at the port of call of no return, lacking in faith unto good works, where faith without works is dead? Am I working out my own salvation with *fear and trembling*? (Phil. 2:12) Or do I have a *false sense of security* because I have boarded the wrong *ship* called the *good ship lollypop* that is docked in the harbor of unbelief and (false doctrine)!"

As for me, I choose to stay on board with Jesus, trusting and believing in him, for I love him, and it now grieves me to be far from him. He will never guide our *ship* to the port of no return. Therefore, I now hold fast to him with both hands and feet.

There are those who will continue to run after star-studded skies on their horizon, for their vision 'has been limited and clouded by their love for the things of this world. If we knew the wisdom of knowing Christ Jesus, then he would be our only vision. Nothing shall be impossible to them who love him, for through the purity of their hearts, others shall see a reflection of him. Oh, what glory he has bestowed upon his church!

Beloved ones, the church is destined to be his glorious church, the crowning glory of her husband, the Lord Jesus Christ (Eph. 5:22–33).

There shall be a (great forsaking) falling away-(2 Thess. 2:1–3). With this in mind, read the parable of the ten young virgins in Matthew 25:1–13. The choice is ours to choose whom we will serve.

Satan 'tempted Jesus, with the 'things of this world, and Jesus defeated him openly with the pure Word of God. (Luke 4:4–12) "It is written that man shall not live by bread alone, but by every word of God ... Get thee behind me, Satan: for it is written, Thou shalt worship the Lord thy God, and him only shalt thou serve... It is said, Thou shalt not tempt the Lord thy God." The Enemy of our souls is inferior, late, slow, and behind us because of the blood of Jesus."

Believe beloved ones. Run with patience the race that our Lord has set before us (Heb. 12:1–29), and run toward the mark for the prize of the high calling in Christ Jesus, which is to obtain an incorruptible crown (1 Cor. 9:24–27). Jesus has made a surer way, because he is now the *only* way, the truth, and the life, and no one comes to the Father except by him. When he comes back for us, there will be no more sorrow or pain.

There is no possibility of revolt in the heavens, for we will be marked with the Holy Spirit and fire, purged by God's love and presented as the prize for his only begotten Son, a crown of glory due him. And we will be without spot or wrinkle to glorify him, transformed by his blood to be pure, whole, and holy, a reflection of Jesus, changed to be just like him.

I am pressing toward the mark for the prize of the high calling of God in Christ Jesus. This calling is to know the Father and to 'be known by him. For he is no respecter of persons, neither is there male or female—only sons, joint heirs with Jesus in the kingdom of God. We will, be conjoined together with the Father, Son, and Holy Spirit, truly and fitly joined together, lacking nothing, for he is the Lord, of our Righteousness.

He is the firstborn of many brethren (sons). Could this be an unveiling of a mystery? All I know is that Jesus is sharing his birthright with me: a woman. In Jesus' day, no man could do that. This 'one thing I am sure of: I do not lack a vision, for his face is always before me. He is all I see. You men who cannot see yourselves as a bride, and you women who cannot see yourselves as a son, get over it! Something wonderful will happen, and we will be changed in the twinkling of an eye.

E. C.

For the Lord of Hosts is calling his remnant home to their Messiah—both Jews and Gentiles. "Now behold, a whirlwind of the Lord is gone forth in fury, even a grievous whirlwind: it shall fall grievously upon the head of the wicked (Jer. 23:1–40). Judgment begins with the house of God as revealed in the book of Revelation in the messages to the seven churches: Ephesus, Smyrna, Thyatira, Pergamos, Sardis, Philadelphia, and Laodicea. He that hath an ear, let him hear what the Spirit saith unto the churches.

Unite in the Holy Spirit and in the power of his resurrection love.

Chapter 8
Dimmer and Dumber

Satan, the enemy of our soul, is astute—wily, full of guile, tricky—and, mostly, *stupid*. He believes his own lie, ever blinded by his own false light, which grows dimmer, dimmer, and dumber. We believe in the Light of the World, our Lord Jesus Christ, and the Word of the living God, and the brightness of his second coming as the Prince of Peace. Thou art worthy, Emmanuel, "God with us," our Shepherd, the living Word, the risen One who will come back for us.

He said he would never leave us or forsake us, that we should trust him because he is preparing a place for us. He has not abandoned us or left us alone. The Holy Spirit is with us. Do you not know that the Father, Son, and Holy Spirit are one? (2 Cor. 2:17).

We have his power, authority, and grace, and it's up to us to utilize it. This is the force and energy to do his work, for the Holy Spirit transfers his energy to us. This is the Holy Spirit's convincing force, the reason he uses the weak to confound the strong—and the wise in their own conceits.

He said it was better to leave earth and send the Comforter to us, but we have put this power on the back burner because it is too hot for our flesh. Therefore, our pride limits us in doing his will and his work on this earth. Yet there are still a few who are willing to yield and respect the authority of the Holy Spirit.

Now we have the force and energy of the Holy Spirit to do his work, for the Holy Spirit transfers his energy to us. This is our birthright (Mark 6:7–13).

Jesus called unto himself the twelve and began to send them forth, two by two, to preach and heal. He gave them power over unclean spirits and commanded them that they should take nothing for their journey, save a staff only—no bread, no money in their purses.

Eight is the number of new beginnings. The number 888 is the numerical value of Jesus. The first new beginning in 888 is Jesus being born as God in the flesh; the second new beginning is his death and resurrection; the third new beginning will be when he comes back to earth for us. There are many Scriptures to verify this. I challenge you to research the number eight in the Word of God for yourself; trust no man's church.

Eight is the octave that Jesus sings his tones pure and melodic. It is a high pitch of excitement, as he awaits his second coming. (An *octave* is (1) a musical interval embracing eight degrees, also a tone or note at this interval or the whole series of notes, tones, or keys within this interval; (2) a group of eight (*Merriam-Webster Dictionary*).

Rejoice and sing with our Lord for one can put a thousand to flight and two, ten thousand.

Now, growl at the Enemy, children, and give him no place, for my grace is sufficient for you (Lev. 14:10; Ex.

22:30; Gen. 5; Gen. 17; 1 Peter 3:20; 1 Peter 3:8; Matt. 27:1; John 20:26).

In the end, every knee shall bow and every tongue confesses that Jesus Christ is Lord—without exception (Isa. 45:23; Rom. 14:11).

Jesus says, "I have chosen twelve to go forth in this hour with my power, for I never change. "I AM that IAM: constant, never changing. You will have to trust in me for all that you have need of, for the love of money is the root of all evil."

Chapter 9
Deep Waters

The Lord's beloved responds to the call of the turtledove. It is a call to lay down her life for her brother, her beloved Lord. With the constant sound of a rushing, mighty wind, a waterfall of love continually flows through her, cleansing and purifying her for his use. Now she can swim with ease through the turbulent waters of life (Ps. 42:1–11).

With clarity of mind, body, soul, and spirit, her way 'is made straight and attainable by her faith, no matter the turmoil around her. Her faith in him is a place of tranquil rest, a peace that surpasses all understanding. No more outer noise filters through to her, only peace, and an inner beauty that comes with great contentment. This heavenly place is a foretaste of the promise of eternal life, which submerges her into the very depths of the river of life that flows with milk and honey. This is a testament of the Lord's unending love for his beloved bride, his church.

As she draws ever closer to him *"deep calls to deep"* at this depth she yields to the Holy Spirit's still, small voice and immerses herself into the *depths* of the *water of life* the Word, which cleanses, renews, and frees her from her past. When this chapter is complete in her life, if she does not faint, she will come forth flowing with love, mercy, and compassion, believing in and experiencing the freedom to walk in the power of his cleansing blood (Ps. 42:7).

Her desire is now to please him and never to sin again, yet the flesh is weak. In addition, she soon finds out that without faith in Jesus Christ it is impossible to please God. She rejoices, for she is no longer alone, as the Word of God accompanies her wherever she goes. She digs *"deep and deeper"* into the Word of God and finds the meat of the Word, where the eyes of her understanding our opened and *'mysteries* are revealed by the Lord's sent one, the precious Holy Spirit.

The Scriptures become alive—simple and clear—as she draws even closer to her Lord. Because of his righteousness, he helps her to overcome each habitual sin. Then, as she willingly and fearlessly draws even closer to her Lord, she becomes more like him and is less likely to sin. If she does sin, it is because she has stepped away from her Lord, so she is quick to repent and draw closer to him once again, for he never leaves her side.

She knows she has an advocate with the Father. The *strength* she needs to walk away from sin and the desire for the things and ways of the world's kingdoms is in and through her Lord Jesus Christ. She has learned that she can do nothing apart from him, and her desire is now for him.

The false lights of this world have become dim to her because of the nearness of Jesus. In knowing and seeing him through the eyes of the Holy Spirit, she sees the kingdoms of this world fade away and become nothing compared to his *luminescent, radiant light* that consumes all his promises and his eternal kingdom promised to those who believe in him (John 3:15–21).

Her *prosperity* is in him and is not limited to the uncertain riches of this world. It flows like living water through her from him, now and forever. "Worthy is the Lamb that was slain to receive power, and riches, and wisdom, and strength, and honor, and glory, and blessing. And every creature which is in heaven, and on the earth, and under the earth, and such as are in the sea, and all that are in them, heard I saying, Blessing, and honor, and glory, and power, be unto him that sited upon the throne, and unto the Lamb for ever and ever" (Rev. 5:12–13).

Let all who believe in the Lamb of God who sits upon the throne say this prayer: "His kingdom come, his will be done on earth as it is in heaven."

For we overcome by the blood of the Lamb and the word of our testimony; and they loved not their lives unto death and we will not love our own lives but will lay them down for our friends, for there is no greater love than to lay our lives down for our brothers. This love will flow through the ones Jesus has chosen out of the world, and the world shall hate them.

Beloved ones do not let go of the Lord, for you cannot *swim upstream* in your own *strength*. Cling to him, for he sent the Holy Spirit to lead and guide you to him. Be encouraged, for you are not alone. Remember this always: the world changes, but he never changes (Heb. 13:8).

Chapter 10
"Disjointed, Not Broken"

The Lord is ever seeking throughout the earth for the true worshippers, those who will worship him in spirit and in truth, the ones who love him. As he sits at the right hand of the Father, ever interceding for them, the Holy Spirit circles the earth, fine tuning the Lord's beloved,. A chosen vessel is she, reflecting the humility of her Lord and Savior Jesus Christ, who was never accepted, always rejected.

She labors on, knowing that her Lord will come back soon, for she senses his presence everywhere—even in the deep recesses and darkness of this world's despair. The clutter of this world has infected the churches like tares among the wheat, and it makes a swishing sound as they grow up together. I hear the sound of angels' wings fluttering overhead, getting ready to separate his bride from the tares.

My heart cries out, "Lord, there's much yet for us to do. There are so many lost, hurting, and dying people, and I have done nothing for you yet.

E. C.

Then I hear my Lord say, "Trust me, dear one, to complete the good work I have begun in you. You, my beloved ones, will do exploits in these last days. For you are chosen by the Father, prepared before the foundations of the world for a time such as this. He has chosen you for me. Fear not, little flock, for I have not lost one sheep, no, not one—except the man of perdition."

Then suddenly, as his Word pours over me, he speaks this to me: "You have not been broken, just disjointed. You will now understand why you 'have been hidden in me. My beloved ones will only recognize each other by the love they have one for another. I wandered the earth without you the first time, willingly laying my life down for you and having no place to rest my head, because my bride, the church, was yet far from me.

"When I come back for you, it will be with a shout. I will no longer groan with the weight of my longing for you. No longer will I proclaim that foxes have holes and the birds of the air have nests but that the Son of Man has nowhere to rest his head. My beloved, my arms long to hold you, for you are my resting place and I am yours. We will come together soon, my beloved, so very soon, for I sense your nearness and you sense mine. When I come back, we will dance in the dark, dispelling, scattering, dissipating the darkness forever. For beloved, you are a chosen generation, a royal priesthood, a holy nation, a peculiar people that will show forth the praises of the Father who has called you out of darkness into his marvelous light.

"My beloved has become divided and separated by the sleight of men, in addition to becoming disjointed by their false doctrine. You were to unify in my name, the name that is above every name, not in the name of your religious organizations or leaders. You have become stiff-necked and are driven by the cares of this world. Come to me, all you who are heavy-laden, and learn of me, and I will give you rest. Unite in my love through the unity of the Holy Spirit. Come, my beloved, come to me, for surely I come quickly as a thief in the night for you."

Comments

Disjointed means (1) incoherent, (2) separated at, or as if at, the joint (Prov. 25:19).

Incoherent means (1) not sticking closely or compactly together; loose; (2) lacking normal clarity or intelligibility in speech or thought (Prov. 18:1–24).

Loose means (1) not rigidly fastened; (2) free from restraint or obligation; (3) not dense or compact in structure; (4) slack, not precise or exact (Prov. 25:2–28).

Lewd means (1) sexually unchaste; also, obscene or vulgar. (These are they who love their own flesh more than they love God and have not crucified the flesh (Gal. 4:5–26).)

Slacken means (1) careless, negligent; (2) not busy or active; (3) sluggish, listless (Prov. 27:1–28).

Chapter 11
Eyes Have Not Seen

Beloved church, as beautiful as the valleys and pastures

That, are flowing with their lush grasses and the scent of wildflowers

Coming off the prairies at sunset,

Or the gentle breezes tumbling softly off the top of ocean waves,

Or the snow-tipped mountains and the immense heavens, as stars twinkle in the night,

Or the beautiful moon that cradles the earth until the morning light,

The soft coo-cooing of the doves as they bed down for the night,

Or a precious newborn baby who coos as its hand reaches out to touch your face.

How precious is a kitten that plays with a ball of yarn or a puppy that yawns as it falls over at the effort he has just made.

There are so many blessings we have taken for granted, no matter our station in life or whether we believe in Jesus or not. We all have these blessings before us, and we are all free to accept or reject the idea that God made them to bless us. As his children, we must finish all that he has placed on our plates—even the vegetables of trials and tribulations—because they are good for us and for his kingdom, and we know that the best promises are yet to come. "Eye hath not seen, nor ear heard, neither have entered into the heart of man, the things which God hath prepared for them that love him" (1 Cor. 2:9).

Sadly, some of us have become spoiled little children who have not learned to hear the voice of their father. Their 'ears have been tickled, by the false ones they want their dessert now, and they get it by attrition, by wearing away their covering of God's Word by friction. If they would just stop complaining, hustling and bustling around—even in the big cities—they would become content in the state they find themselves in and would see the wonders our Creator made for us, for he takes care of his own. Yet all they want is prosperity, prosperity from the kingdoms of this world; and this is all they desire—instead of him.

The prosperity of God's kingdom is not of this world, for eyes have not seen, nor ears heard what God has prepared for those that love him. He is our faithful Lord Jesus Christ, the wonder of all wonders. How can we pray for the wandering, lost, lonely souls if we do not know him? By our own examples they should know, whether they believe in him or not, that they are his creation and he loves them.

The wonder of God's loving essence- enfolds embraces and blesses us 'all mankind, with compassion creating a perfume of his love. Our future and our hope are in him, as is the hope that one day we will have the ability to create in unison to rule and reign with him. Rev. 20: 4 *Unison sameness or identity in musical pitch<sing in unison> harmonious agreement or union: "ONE-ACCORD.* If we are willing to draw close to him through his graciousness towards us, then 'we and the world will see him as he really is.

Are 'we grateful for his mercy that endures forever, or are we bound to the kingdoms and treasures of this world with their feel-good, look-at-me aspects? That makes no sense to his kingdom ways and sensibilities because it means there tainted by an I-want-it-all-now attitude. Some say they do not know why God wants them rich and not poor.

This philosophy has made the church lethargic, noncompliant to God's will and authority. Such people are no longer of any use to God and his kingdom, for they have fallen asleep and are no longer actively walking by faith. Some who profess to know him do not speak his Word in and out of season. No one wants to suffer for the gospel's sake anymore, so 'they leave their first love, to become puppets pumped up by the hot air of the world's words, which have no lasting effect or power to save them.

Therefore, they become 'defeated and deflated in the heat of battle. They have to reread their books over, and over, watch TV, or return to their conferences in order to 'be pumped up again with hot air—until their balloons pop!

They continue to conjure up one formula after another. Like mad, scientists or little gods, they seek to create gold for prosperity, following one another's twisted words, ways, and formulas, or a combination thereof, rather than following God's ways, which are higher than man's ways.

In the end, all these false ones' endeavors may create the gold of prosperity, but it will be fool's gold and a fool's prosperity: a counterfeit. Such gain comes from the people they fleece, and it will pass away, for they have changed God's Word, as did their Father of Lies in the Garden of Eden. Such words tickle the ears; they sound right, but they are so wrong. It is all hype; it stimulates the senses, producing false hopes and vain visions and images. It deceives, selling a bill of goods to people who cannot see what they are really buying.

When the world's formula does not work for someone, these false ones blame that person for applying it wrong. They point to themselves and say to a captive audience, "It works for me." Then they hold up the Bible for the whole world to see—and it *does* work for them, because they steal, kill, and destroy to keep it working for them. They are deluded like the Father of Lies who desires to be equal to God. Beware what and whom you believe, church, for Revelation 3:11 states, "Behold, I come quickly: hold that fast which thou hast, that no man takes thy crown."

I believe that the parable of the ten young virgins (Matt. 25:1–13) is symbolic of both Israel's true converts and the Lord's Gentile bride, and much of this mystery is yet to 'be revealed. The Lord is talking about the kingdom of God, saying that there will be some wise ones who are anointed, with the Word of God, who wait for the Lord Jesus Christ. They know him and hear his voice. In addition, there will be some 'foolish ones, who have not prepared themselves with the washing of the water of the Word by the Holy Spirit so that their oil might be full as the Lord tarries.

These five foolish—naturally and spiritually—ones will slumber and sleep, and then they will wake up and find that their oil is running out. They will seek to find the oil, but they will be unable to find it. At the midnight hour just before dawn, just before the daystar rises, which is symbolic of the Lord's second coming, there will be a shout. Then all the virgins who trimmed their lamps and 'were anointed by the Word, those who watched and waited and were prepared, will open the door when he knocks.

It is not an easy thing to walk parallel to Jesus, to pick up our cross daily and follow him. However, as we do, his grace will abound in us, transforming us from glory to glory until his return for us, and when we see him, we will become like him. Now, rejoice, beloved church, rejoice, for all things are possible with God.

One day is like a thousand years and a thousand years as one day to him. Therefore, in one day, by divine promise, his beloved bride, his church, will put on Christ Jesus, and we will become his beloved wife, his crowning glory, for the wife is the glory of her husband. Because his love has become the breadth, length, depth, and height of her love for him, he is her prosperity, and he will fulfill her highest achievement to become his crowning glory.

In the beginning, the whole earth was full of God's glory, for he knew his church before the foundations of the earth. This is God's faith; he never goes by what he sees, hears, or feels, for he is the Creator of heaven and earth, and he creates everything by divine design. You are his divine-glory church. Please look up the whole definition of *design* and be as wowed as I was.

Let me speak forth the mystery of a counterfeit pearl that has formed in the midst of God's beloved church. This one casts her pearls before dogs and swine, and she is a hypocrite, an obvious pretender who has deliberately rejected the message of the truth. She is a tare that hides among the wheat, and she is leaven that the Enemy, the Devil, has planted among the good wheat.

The "pearl of great price" is his goodly pearl, who proclaims, "His kingdom come, his will be done on earth as it is in heaven." She has forsaken all to follow him, but she will never love to the extent that God loves her, for he is God. However, she will be a reflection of him, and the world will hate her as it did her Lord Jesus (Matt 7:6; 13:45–46).

The false-pearl harlot in the church hides behind her elegant clothing and jewelry, showing her wealth and false attractiveness, drawing attention to herself by emotional, aesthetic, or artistic appeal. She is a caricature, a distorted representation of his true-pearl church.

This harlot spirit can be male or female, and it comes forth especially in literature, where it artfully distorts the truth and has the qualities of a caricature. She has become ridiculous in her appearance, and everything she puts her hands to has aesthetic appeal. This attracts and places others in a lethargic condition, as men lust after her and women desire to be her. Wealth, power, and fame are her desire in this life and the next. Boy' is she in for a rude awakening!

E. C.

The spirit of the harlot makes way for the Antichrist, and she is forceful in her energetic, hypnotic ways. As she sells people a bill of goods, her false piety, strength, gentleness, and happiness will readily hold people's attention and draw them away from forming a personal relationship with the Lord Jesus Christ.

She is counterproductive to God's kingdom, for her desire is for the things and kingdoms of this world and its approval. She pivots from one gender to the other, altering her persona. Spiritually, she exaggerates herself and confuses, just as Satan did in the garden of Eden (Rev. 17:1–18). She is the harlot spirit, the opposite of God's Holy Spirit. There is neither male nor female in God's kingdom, nor is there any confusion, for his bride knows who she is in Christ Jesus. This harlot spirit changes, but God never changes.

"For the kingdom of God is 'not just meat and drink; but righteousness, and peace, and joy in the Holy Ghost." (Rom. 14:17) "For God hath not given us the spirit of fear; but of power and of love, and of a sound mind. Be not thou therefore not ashamed, of the testimony of our Lord, nor of me, his prisoner: but be thou partakers of the afflictions of the gospel, according to the power of God. Who hath saved us, and called us with a holy calling, not according to our works, but according to his own purpose and grace, which was given to us in Christ Jesus before the world began. But is now made manifest by the appearing of our Savior Jesus Christ, who hath abolished death, and hath brought life and immortality to light through the gospel" (2 Tim. 1:7–10). May the God of peace rule our hearts.

This is a call to arms for the church to unite in the power of his love, for when we do unify, revival will break forth.

"The banner over us is his love, and we are as terrible as an army with banners" when we are in unison with him (Songs 2:4; 6:4). The Lord is saying for the third time, "If you love me, then feed my lambs."

He is not a movement or denomination, and if you think your religious movement is the only way, I must remind you that *Jesus* is the only way, *the* truth, and *the* life. No man comes to the Father but by him. Then, if you still think your way is the only way, remember that he has come to set the captives free. His ways are higher than our ways.

In spite of us and because of his grace, I believe that we who love the Lord will all have something to bring to his banqueting table. In the end, he will judge us all when we stand before him. In all of this, he is saying, "You are either for me or against me. Hear this and hear well, for he is preparing us to unite in the unity of the Holy Spirit and the resurrection power of his love."

Then revival will break forth in his church, for he is not willing that any man should perish. His resurrection power is not something spooky; it is his love working through us, and it revives us. A resurrected life is one that is free from dead works, one where a person has died to self so that others might live. It is a new beginning.

Love is the Master's master key, and forgiveness is the oil that releases this key to open all doors. Take heed: even the Enemy realizes that God must and does unite his followers. Stand tall, America, for the battle lines are being drawn. United we stand; divided we fall. This is a turning point for America. God has blessed her, and now

E. C.

it is time to take back what the Enemy has stolen from her—freedom and her God-given right to choose.

Stop giving place to the Enemy, for he is a liar and the truth is not in him. We are still a Christian nation, so send the Enemy packing into a distant country with his tail between his legs. The Lord has chosen a man for this hour. Will he heed this call? We will see. He is a man after God's own heart, putting God first above all others, even above his own desires and promises, a man who will unite rather than divide this country, and he is struggling with his decision. How do I know this? Because I prayed, and the Lord answered me: the gates of hell shall not prevail against God's church. Oh beloved ones, we have not because we ask not or because we ask amiss.

I am happy to say I was raised Catholic, but I learned and was blessed by so many other denominations. For I saw in some of them, how much their members loved the Lord; they just expressed it differently from me. We are not perfect, because the tares are among us; yet we are to strive to be perfect, as our Father in heaven is perfect. All denominations are far from perfect, just like the Catholic Church.

We are one body of the Lord Jesus Christ but different members, who are disjointed and trying to be the whole body. We are separated and divided because of the sin of pride. We must obey God rather than man. Please note that I am not part of any ministry or promoting any denomination; I am a Christian and a follower of my Lord.

I am just a seventy-year-old woman who loves the Lord and her country of America. Please hear what the spirit is saying to the churches. Fight for your Christian values, and vote for the man who has them, no matter his denomination. I humbly confess, as Paul did, that I know nothing and am nothing without my Lord Jesus Christ (1 Cor. 1:31).

If you are wondering why I sign as I do, "The Pearl of Great Price," it is for the same reason that I call myself a Christian and have been doing so for many, many years: I simply believe that I am who he says I am. The logo of "The Pearl of Great Price" was given to me by inspiration of the Holy Spirit.

The church is a many-membered body and thus is like a strand of pearls. When we are together in the unity of the faith in spirit, we will be that single, priceless pearl, the bride that is soon to be the wife of our Lord Jesus Christ. Stop calling good evil and evil good, and discern the times. Remember that Satan smiles and call his lies truth, and he always blames others as Adam blamed Eve.

Chapter 12
Be Encouraged

This is a time of great introspection, when we look inward at the intents of the heart. We are not in competition with each other but are predestined to finish the race together. We are to stay humble before our Lord, for no flesh shall glory in His presence. We are the few that have chosen him, and we are pieces of his divine puzzle, his body, placed together for his end-time purposes. If this is so, then we are in heavenly places with him. I want to make a note hear that my writing "His Devine Puzzle" was used by another giving no glory to the Lord so I will not use it here, I delight in giving you the glory my King

God is rich in mercy, and the great love wherewith he loved us, even when we were dead in sins, hath quickened us together with Christ. He has raised us up together and made us sit in heavenly places in Christ Jesus, that in the ages to come he might show the exceeding riches of his grace in his kindness toward us through Christ Jesus. For, we are 'saved by grace, through faith that works by love, and not of ourselves. It is the gift of God, not of works, lest any man should boast. For we are his workmanship, created in Christ Jesus unto good works, which God has before ordained that we should walk in (Eph. 2:4–10).

There is great danger in lifting up yourself or anyone else in this hour. Beloved, if you are picking up your cross daily and following Jesus but you are proclaiming to the body of Christ and to the Lord, "Look what *I* have done for you," then you are not dead to self yet. Remember that the dead in Christ shall rise first and that the first shall be last and the last first, for God saves the best for last (1 Thess. 4:16; Matt. 19:30; John 2:9–11).

Boasting in any form is not Christ like. The Scripture that comes to mind is the one where the rich young ruler called Jesus "good." The Lord asked him, "Why do you call me good, when there is no one good save one, and that is God?" (Luke 18:18–30). Did you ever wonder at these words? I did, and this was what I heard: *The Father and I are one, Evelyn, and we cannot do anything apart from one another.*

Our Lord was giving honor where honor was due, and that was to the Father. Jesus was still in the flesh, and he knew that no flesh, could glory in the holy God's presence—not even his precious Son who was without sin.

There is now help in the Holy Spirit. If we walk in the Spirit, we will not fulfill the lusts of the flesh. Do you hunger and thirst after him or after fame, wealth, and the accolades of men of this world?

We must put first the kingdom of God and his righteousness, and then all these other things shall be added unto us. When you reach this point, nothing else will matter but his will. All honor, glory, and praise be to the Father, Son, and Holy Spirit (Matt. 6:33).

Chapter 13
Opposites Attract

(Genesis 1:1–5)

In the beginning, God created the heavens and the earth. In addition, the earth was without form and void, and darkness was upon the face of the deep. As the Spirit of God moved upon the face of the waters, God moved on the surface, the outward appearance of the water. He went deep and then rose to the dark surface. *He will do the same in this hour.*

I believe that Lucifer and his fallen angels 'were cast to earth because it was without form and void, for God had a plan, a sure way to destroy the Enemy from the beginning.

Moreover, God said, "Let there be light," and there was light. Then God saw the light that it was good; and God divided the light from the darkness. *He will do the same in this hour.* God called the light *day*, and the darkness he called *night*. In addition, the evening and the morning were the first day.

Being total opposites of one another, the Enemy will be drawn to God like a moth to a flame, and God's love shall consume his Enemy: Satan, the adversary, the Dragon, the Serpent, the clever tempter, the slanderer, the counterfeiter who deceives the whole world. God will forever torment him by exposing his lies with the truth. For God's love is a consuming fire. *So shall it be in this hour.*

For God, who is good, makes a distinction between "good" light and "evil" darkness. The light is God's beloved Son, with whom the Father is well-pleased (Matt. 19:17). "And this voice which came from heaven we heard, when we were with him in the holy mount. We have also a more sure word of prophecy; whereunto ye do well that ye take heed, as unto a light that shineth in a dark place, until the day dawn, and the daystar arise in your hearts: knowing this first, that no prophecy of the scripture is of any private interpretation. For the prophecy came not in old time by the will of man: but holy men of God spake as they were moved by the Holy Ghost" (2 Peter 1:18–21). *So shall it be in this hour.*

In the beginning, God divided the good light from the evil darkness, for Lucifer had been cast out of heaven, deep into the earth's core. Therefore, shall it be once again for eternity (Rev. 20:7–14). God's light is good. "I am the light of the world: he that followeth me shall not walk in darkness, but shall have the light of life" (John 8:12). In the beginning, Jesus was the light of the world. Let us now walk as children in the purity of his holy light, not calling evil good and good evil.

May all praise, honor, and glory go to the Father, Son, and Holy Spirit! All creation will rejoice at his second coming, no longer moaning and groaning, waiting for the manifested sons of God for old things shall pass away, and all things become new. Now Jesus is the firstborn of many brethren (Rom. 8:29). Jesus never once suggested one way or another to be *equal* to God but to be *one* with the Father. The Father, Son, and Holy Spirit are one, and the beloved 'are called to be one with them.

To the firstborn son, Jesus, belongs the birthright, which includes the headship of the family or tribe and a double portion of his Father's property. Jesus has the headship of the family of God. Jesus is the head of the body, the church—not man. If we believe that Jesus is the Son of God, then we must believe that we are joint heirs with Christ Jesus (Rom. 8:17). Now, beloved of God, read Romans 8:1–39 and rejoice!

May the double portion of his blessings overtake you as you study to make yourself approved as a worker for God. Be about the Father's business, for we are predestined to be in the unity of the Holy Spirit for his glory. Humbly find your place in the beloved, and do not break ranks, for we are to walk together in the unity of our faith in our Lord Jesus Christ.

We must fight the good fight of faith, holding each other's hands. We need each other in order to be, fitly joined together, becoming one with the head of the church, our Lord Jesus Christ. We are not broken, but we 'are disjointed and scattered by man's false pride, which has caused division.

Opposites attract. We are all part of a many-membered body that has different parts in order to function properly. We 'were made to 'complement one another. We 'were never meant to compete with one another. Just as the natural right and left sides of the body, need each other to function properly, so do the spiritual right and left sides of the body in Christ. We are all a part of our Lord's body, and we must move and have our being in him, for apart from him we can do nothing for the kingdom of God.

You who think you are in charge of his sheepfold are moving with your own personal charm and worldly attributes to compete with one another, seducing others to become just like you—or worse than you are. Leading others to stray from the faith, you are always a tear in his body, for you never knew God. You have 'been planted by the Enemy to cause confusion, for birds of a feather that flock together, picking and devouring the young wheat. Your desire is to pump each other up with false interpretations of God's Word.

Seducing others to be more and more like the world, you shall pass away. You rightly say you are little gods, for your god is the god of this world. In your Hollywood ways, you have portrayed Jesus as man of beauty; yet while he was on this earth, he was a man of sorrows, not comely in appearance. You have created a false image of him. In essence, you have created your own following instead of leading the children to follow Jesus.You have suffered the children to come unto me, offending my little ones, and now it is better that a millstone be hung around your neck and you be cast into the sea. *And so shall it be in this hour* (1 Tim. 6:1–21; Matt. 19:14; Mark 9:42).

The Enemy tempts you, drawing you to the kingdoms of this world and all its riches, giving you his god complex so that you will follow Lucifer, the sun of the morning. He will speedily disappear before the rising sun: God's only begotten Son. Jesus came to set us free to choose whom we will serve, giving us a better promise of his kingdom to come. His will be done, on earth as it is in heaven (Matt. 4:1–11).

The Lord will never dominate us, for he is meek and lowly and has set us free to choose to rule and reign with him—or not. He is not, nor can he be, different denominations. He alone has the power—not man—to designate, choose, and know who his beloved is, for she is everywhere, even as she is hidden in him. Herein is a mystery, and the whole earth is full of his glory (Col. 3:1–11). God's beloved fallows him her beautiful bright and morning star and his promise of a new day. She waits patiently with her lamp full of oil for his promised return, for she is chosen but not yet installed.

Comments

Opposite means "the other of a matching or contrasting pair."

You will reflect the false light of the kingdoms of this world, or you will reflect the kingdom of God and the true Light of the World, his Son.

Attract means "to draw to or toward" oneself, God, or mammon.

God is everywhere and in everything. We cannot separate God from his creation, for everything that was, ever made, was made by him. (Acts 17:24).

God is good, and he has no fellowship with darkness or evil. Therefore, we who are his own are to dispel evil with the good news. Thus, we honor the blood sacrifice of his only begotten Son, Jesus Christ, who openly defeated the Enemy at the cross and delivered us from the law of sin and death, freeing us from the sting of death. "Oh death,

E. C.

where is your sting? O grave, where is thy victory?" (1 Cor. 15:35–58). Praise him; praise him; praise his holy name, oh ye his holy people and all ye creation. From the beginning, God set up the Enemy to be defeated with his goodness.

Thank you, precious Holy Spirit, for the inspired Word of God.

Chapter 14
In His Time

This is the mystery of the "pearl of great price," as it 'was explained to me by the Holy Spirit.

Jesus left the security of his heavenly home, where he was sitting at the right hand of the Father, Jesus chose to come to earth to set 'his chosen few free from the law of sin and death. Many 'were called but few would choose him. Therefore, Jesus came to earth for the few who would willingly choose to fallow him "The Pearl of Great Price" his hidden treasure. This treasure is far more precious to him than silver or gold or all the glories of his heavenly kingdom.

He willingly laid down his life, coming to earth in the likeness of man, to fulfill and obtain a greater promise: the unveiling of his hidden treasure—his bride, the church—she is fearfully and wonderfully made (Ps. 139:14; Isa. 45:3; Matt. 6:21; Luke 12:34).

The glory he left behind when he came to earth dimmed, paled in the sight of the promised glory of his beloved wife-church. The price he paid for his promised bride, his beloved church, was a transfusion of his life-giving blood, his DNA, his divine nature and authority. The breath of life that was given to Adam in the beginning—and to Eve, who was bone of Adam's bone and flesh of his flesh—was not enough to complete the promise of eternal life, because Adam was not God, and he would sin.

This promise, from the foundation of the world, was given to Adam and Eve by the Father, and the Father was not a man that he should lie. Therefore, our Lord Jesus came to earth for us to fulfill his promise of eternal life, and he made an open show of the Enemy. For that old, lying Serpent, Lucifer, the "son of the morning," deceived Adam and Eve, coming to them as an angel of light. Lucifer, the deceiver knew full well that Jesus Christ was the Light of the World, the "bright and morning star."

Yes, Jesus and Lucifer were close, yet far apart from one another, and Lucifer was able to deceive Adam and Eve (Isa. 45:7). I pondered this verse in Isaiah, and I believe I understand the meaning of these words in Proverbs 16:4: "The Lord has made all things for himself: yea, even the wicked for the day of evil."

Satan was, originally created as one of God's highest angels, not to *be* evil but *for the day of* evil—not to be the first practitioner of sin. However, Satan deceived himself into thinking that he was above God his Creator, causing some of the angels in heaven to rebel. Satan is still causing rebellion by deceiving the world with a counterfeit of the Word of God. He is a liar, and the truth is not in him.

God created Lucifer and only God could destroy him and all his works even death. 1Cor.15:25—26. Satan is so deluded that he refuses to see that he 'was defeated by the living word Gods only begotten Son, our Lord Jesus Christ.

Man and angels alike 'were created with free will. The difference between us is that man 'was created in both the image and likeness of God. Satan hates us because we have a soul, because Father God breathed life into man, and he became a living soul. Rejoice, for our Lord Jesus Christ, the only begotten Son of the living God, has set us free. What man could not do alone, Jesus did for us by coming to earth as the Son of Man, being born of a virgin, and dying on the cross for the sins of all who would believe in him.

He proclaimed with his last breath that the job was finished. His promise to you and me is *yes* and *amen*. He will complete the good work he has begun in us. In Revelation 22:13, he proclaimed, "I am Alpha and Omega, the beginning and the end, the first and the last. Now, I ask you, does that sound like there is anything too hard for him? This was a mystery hidden in the tablets of the Holy Spirit's heart for a time such as this.

The parable of the hidden treasure is in Matthew 13. "All these things spoke Jesus unto the multitude in parables; and without a parable spoke he not unto them: That it might be fulfilled which was spoken by the prophet, saying, I will open my mouth in parables; I will utter things which have been kept secret from the foundation of the world" (Matt. 13:34–36). A small portion of the mystery of the pearl of great price is revealed within these pages.

Love's Imprint

Father, as you turned the pages of eternity, your Son Jesus is 'revealed as your truth, which came forth to those who understood and accepted this fine printing of your will through your great grace, mercy, and love. Forever you sustain them, imprinting their hearts with your love, not written with tablets of ink but by the hand of the Holy Spirit.

They delight to do your will, for your laws are 'forever written on their hearts. By the drawing closer to you, Lord, the imprinting of your love goes deeper and deeper into the abyss of immeasurable depth, forever burning and pulsating with the consuming fire of your love, branding our hearts forever.

This spiritual and natural journey is rapturously drawing us into your embrace for eternity. Thank you, glorious Holy Father. Thank you for sending your beloved Son to free us from the wages of sin and death in this life and the next. Lord Jesus, thank you for sending the Holy Spirit to lead and guide us to you. Thank you, blessed Holy Spirit, for putting up with us, as most of us dismiss you, grieve you, fail to respect you, and refuse all that you have to offer us.

Because of your great love for us, you continue to gently teach us, showing us the way to the truth and the life that we must lead in you. For this I humbly thank you, for illumination comes from sitting at the feet of Jesus, embracing his cross, picking up our own crosses daily, and following him, thus becoming his living manuscript of his love (2 Cor. 3:1–18).

Now, look up, beloved church, for our redemption draws near in spite of us (Luke 21:28).

We give you all the honor, glory, and praise, Father, Son, and Holy Spirit.

The definition of *imprint* is "to fix firmly, as on the memory, an indelible, distinguishing effect, or influence" (*Merriam-Webster Dictionary*).

As I end this book, take heart, for our beloved Jesus is the God of love that passes all understanding. Moreover, his ways are so much higher than our ways. We cannot love as he does, for 'we are flawed at best. Because of sin, our spots and wrinkles are still with us. Please understand that the Holy Spirit cleanses and purifies us with the washing of the water of the Word, which is Jesus, and (I cannot say this enough) as we draw close to him, we will become more and more like him.

The manifestation of the sons of God will come as we his bride-church, our made known manifest to reflect him, as the blood of Jesus covers our sins. Therefore, the favor of Father God rests on us, so that we 'will not be judged by God. Jesus is now our judge and Redeemer, and he will judge the living and the dead.

The word *manifest* means "readily perceived by the senses and esp. by sight; easily understood; obvious." The verb form means, "To make evident or certain by showing or displaying," e.g., when God *manifests* his power.

Reflect means "to bend or cast back," e.g., when we *reflect*, giving all glory to God. In essence, we give credit where credit is due: all glory and honor to the Father, Son, and Holy Spirit. As we decrease and he increases in us, we will esteem others better than our-selves. Then one day we will become just like him in the twinkling of an eye. We will reflect either Jesus or the world, and it will be evident, for the Lord's beauty comes from within us.

Go in peace, and walk in his most holy love.

Chapter 15
Tree of Life

Gen. 2: 15-16; Rev. 22: 1-2

As we grow in the knowledge of God's kingdom, we will prosper in the *economy* of Christ Jesus in this life, and the next, because we are drawing close to the *source of all life,* our Lord Jesus Christ who is the living word of God the living tree of life. Then as we draw close to Jesus putting Gods' kingdom first and his righteousness then all these other, things 'shall be added unto us. For from the beginning we have always had free will to do God's will, or not, to do his will. Blocked from the tree of life because of the *willful* original sin of Adam and Eve in the Garden of Eden we now have free access to the *tree of life* once again through the blood sacrifice of our Lord Jesus Christ. (*Economy thrifty and efficient use of resources,* The Lords beloved, not limited by this world economy for Jesus is her source)

You cannot just say you accept God's son as your savior and live your life as you please, void of fallowing the Lords teaching. Jesus simple prayer was "Our Father who art in heaven holy be thy name thy kingdom come thy will be done on earth as it is in heaven, give us this day are daily bread and forgive us are sin's as we forgive others and lead us not into temptation but deliver us from evil".

I want to ask you a question; do you think that when Jesus died for our sins it exempts all who have accepted Jesus as there savior from obeying the Fathers Ten Commandments?

I cannot speak for others, but I can tell you this, since I fell in love with Jesus any sin in my life become vary distasteful to me! As I drew closer and closer to him, I became 'greatly convicted of the sin in my life for sin is contrary to who the Father, Son, and Holy Spirit are. Therefor I began to realize that my flesh would not, or could not, glory in his presents and anyone who tried grieved me, to no end I became upset if any persons tried taking credit or to glory in His' presents! For instance, when I shared a word or writing with someone especially the ones in leadership, they would take it and make it their own omitting the vessel the Lord blessed with it in the first place, not giving the glory to the Lord and what he is doing with in the body of Christ! Then as I studied to make myself, approved a-workmen unto God I knew without question why and with greater and greater conviction I earnestly had to repent for my sins, I could not just mouth the words, for repentances would have to come from my heart! Then as the Holy Spirit would lead and guide me through the word, I knew I would once again have clear access to the Father through repentance and placed me back under the cleansing blood of Jesus safe again and under his divine protection. Now my understanding was open to perceive why sin in my life would leave me venerable to the enemy's attack!

Because the habitual sin in my life was causing me too *willfully* 'come out from the safety and covering of the blood of Jesus and I would be subjected and bombarded with a greater attack from the enemy, because we cannot serve two masters!

Baby Christens no matter their age are the most variable if not armed with the whole armor of God, they must be fed the pure word of God first the milk then the meat of the word-no matter their age. My experience was the enemy tried to confuse me with a false gospel, which 'was confess this and that' and you will get this and that, prosperity, and seed faith message! Believe me I know from personal experiences that the enemy will push you back into the world if not *'lovingly* bathed and comforted, with the holy whole word of God. For in *Gods kingdom iron sharpens iron only when tempered with God's love.* For sin leaves, a residue on our flesh and it is there for everyone to see, as we give it to the Holy Spirit to clean us up...were not to *judge after the flesh* but the spirit for many reasons! The most important reason is that only the washing of the water of the word can cleans us of all unrighteousness renewing not only are spirit but are flesh to become the salt of the earth, allowing are light to glow brighter and brighter as we renew are minds daily!

If loving Christians filled with wisdom of God's word are not the ones nurturing baby Christian's *"for they are tender plants easily broken"* then these babies are in for great heartache, backsliding, and stumbling on the way! Because the enemies is a liar and once were born again, free from a particular sin or sins he will be relentless accusing you falsely repeatedly over, and over again of being guilty of the sin that you have been delivered from, The accuser will try and drive you back into it with false accusations! Until we learn to give him no place. Eph. 6:12.

As we mature in our faith by the grace of God, we will understand anger and resentment promotes un-forgiveness along with the *blame game* that is still alive and well in us! (Adam was the first bully for he blamed Eve) As we mature in the word of God we will see, that love is the key to overcoming anger, resentment and bathing in God's love promotes *forgiveness* this is the *wisdom of God's love* for Jesus said the test of a true disciple is to love one another. If we walking in his love then we will bear much fruit! Moreover, I believe, the fruit-love-we are to bear in this life and the next comes from our humble willingness to bare-share are handpicked fruit from the *tree of life* our Lord Jesus Christ which is the love he has shed abroad in our hearts. Now armed with the knowledge of our Lord Jesus Christ we are now ready to share our willingness to summit to his will and then we are able to spread the seed of his love throughout the world "The Gospel of our Lord Jesus Christ." We cry for revival send revival Lord and the Father hears us, but we do not hear him, for he is calling us to *repent, repent* from are wicked ways!

Yet, there is a remnant that will hear him it is his beloved bride in waiting for she is waiting with her oil full for she has willingly been prepared from the foundations of the world for a time such as this for the whole earth is full of God's glory. In addition, the only fruit we can pick from the *tree of life* and the only good seed were called to plant is his-LOVE-not Money! For God so loved the world

E. C.

that he feely gave his only begotten son that whosoever believe in him shall have eternal life.

For beloved, it is impossible to please God without faith for faith works by-love. I rest my case and take exception against all those who would plant any other seed and call it the gospel of our Lord Jesus Christ! The money (changers) prosperity, so called wisdom preachers Ponzi scammers thy all call it seed faith and they always want your seed-faith money! They say If what your believing God for is not coming to pass in your life you need to give them more of your money and you will be blessed, or you are not applying "there word" properly emphasizing they must get their message to the world! I have *"good news"* for theses false ones the world already has their message and it has not working or is it setting them free! Theses false ones are in great bondage to the things of this world, relying solely on this world system to make them 'happy now' and there disciples with vigor defend them...just as the fallen angles defended Lucifer!

Personally, I have just learned to live by faith and not sight and through the things, I have suffered. And theses so called prosperity word of faith preachers should try it, it works' for the longer I live by faith the more content I have become in the state I find myself in like Paul abased or abound. No longer am I run running here or there to this conference or mega church seeking a word from the Lord' buying this-book or that-book' or wanting to 'feel good look at me' running after the I must feel good about me gospel! Because I have learned to lean on my Lords *shoulder*-which is the place of *strength* trusting, and believing in my Lord Jesus Christ because I know him and hear him...now I am able to dismiss and turn away from any other gospel preached. I no longer have to defend the Gospel of my Lord Jesus Christ for it is self-evident as his light shines in you and me. As, we grow in his *grace* and *wisdom* this is the finished work of our Lord Jesus Christ, for he is the author and finisher of our faith. No longer do I question what is happing for I trust him, fear is far from me, and no longer do I question his love for me, for I know I am, *accepted* just as I am into the beloved. Oh, my God thank you!

Time is so very, very short Church as we measure time, for we have much to do before he takes us home. Will you be one of the 'chosen few out of the ten young virgins or are you one of the five left behind (*five is the number of grace*) It is up to you-your choice do not frustrate the *grace* of God. We justify are meanness towards one another by misusing scripture for instance Iron sharpens iron! Prov. 27: 17 However, the Holy Spirit has taught me I 'must be changed, in to his *love vessel an instrument of his Love* before I am qualified to *sharpen iron* in Gods kingdom! For in Gods kingdom *iron sharpens iron* 'only when, tempered with God's love for his love is a consuming fire that does not burn us up for he is in the fire with us, and transforms us into pure gold with his love allowing the dross to fall off with each firing. Again I say stop calling good evil and evil good do you not know what spirit you are of call it what it is sin, all mankind is tempered with God's love and mercy epically the household of God for he is no respecter of persons and have called us all to repentance and to embrace the cross of our Lord Jesus Christ.

I want to reaffirm something hear, by "thanking you Holy Spirit for leading guiding me in to the truth. I 'was raised in a Catholic home I learned to pray and reverence the Father, Son, and Holy Spirit and yes even the Virgin Mary and how to give my offerings. As I learned about other Christian denomination and that, they considered us a cult it puzzled me. As I grew in the word, I found out that no not one is righteous before God and we all fall short for all denominations were and are being exposed to the light of the Word and there darkness was and is being exposed, yes even the Catholic! We are all as filthy rags. When you are tempted to say, our way, is the only way! I must remind you that Jesus is the only way! We become so head strong and willful that the church splits up into different groups, call each other cults, and use the part of the word that works for them! We are so divided no wonder the world does not believe us that Jesus is the only way. Let the Lord Judge those who profess to know him for he will turn to them and says I know you not!

The next time you or I judge someone I pray God reveals what we have hidden in our dark closet or attic. *(Closet is symbolic of things hidden and attic is symbolic of the brain)* This self-righteous behavior has suffered the children to come unto him! I would still be stumbling around in confusion wondering who was right if not for the Holy Spirit who set me free as I studied the word of God for myself. For man, judges after the flesh not the spirit only God can judge the heart, the test of a true disciple is the love they have for one another. But make no mistake your flesh reflects your *stinking thinking* I have been in many churches and this one thing holds true we are all the same, sinners. Well they believe this or that' you say, you' who have such great knowledge of God' and walk perfect before him this is all I know, that Jesus is the only way and we are to love one another as he loves us...are your churches full of the lost hurting dying of this world ya and even those who persecute and despitefully use you. For ya even I love the base things of this world like you-my love! As I draw *closer* and *closer* to him there is less of me more of him, it is great' the bondages just fall off as I draw close to him! WE all fall so short of his glory and if we would get our *SELF* out of the way, and let His Love work, in us we would see revival in the land. It is too simple just to love as 'he dose and hard to obey his commandment to love one another. We with the beam in are eye are so ready to cast the first stone were so out of balance what foolishness.

I pray you will glean from this book through the many facets and veins I have shared with you...from the first to last pages of this book it is a simple message turn from mammon and return to the Father God. This, is his plea' 'warning to his prodigal sons to return home, for the unfolding-of "His Priceless Pearl" is hear and when she is revealed there will be no question who she is. For the angels are coming to separate the tares from the wheat she is humble and obvious for her light shins so bright that it glorifies her Father in heaven. *Surprise* all you denominations she is hidden in him and she is everywhere. *(She is in every denomination and then some no man shall get the glory for her, she is neither male or female)*

"The Parable in Jesus prayer revealed...Luke 11:1-4"

The simple seven points and guidelines in this prayer that 'was given by Jesus are all so very simple yet profound that it pass all understanding and would have stayed a mystery to me without the Holy Spirit guidance...thank you beloved Holy Spirit all glory to you.

1. Primarily Jesus honors the Fathers Holiness.
2. He acknowledges that God's will is sovereign on earth as it is in heaven.
3. We are to live by faith and not by sight for our daily bread for (Jesus is the bread of life).
4. We are to ask for forgiveness of our sins.
5. We are to be aware that if we do not forgive others 'we will not be forgiven.
6. This is a plea to the Holy Spirit to lead us away from temptation by guiding us through the word of God.
7. By complying understanding, obeying the truth and by the combination of this prayer, (but) becomes a condition and are choice to be delivered, or not delivered from evil leaving are free will intact.

How beautiful is the "Holy Word of God-the only good Seed-Jesus Christ" the only way to the *Tree of Life*" now, I am ever excited' expecting to receive more and more revelation of the living word of God in this life and for eternity. I cannot say it enough I'm so excited as I decrease and he increases for his love and forgiveness is without measure. By his *grace* and *mercy,* he is teaching me to love just like him and I know I will never graduate from this class for it takes eternity to complete this course! For he is God and I am his beloved *student servant* and forever *humble* before him for I know my place in him I am just like him for I am my beloveds and he is mine. I am free yet I am willing forever bound to him.

I cry why me' Holy Spirit that you would grace my life with your favor opening up Holy Scripture to me a women with little education and a learning disability? Beloved if you knew what he has forgiven me, then you would understand my cry and know how much this scripture applies to me! I Cor. 1: 18-31. Now I grasp the meaning that there is hope for all, no matter our sins for no sin is little, or big to God for sin is sin being so self-righteous by saying well I never committed that sin and the Lord says pew to you and there is nothing too hard for him. For behold says the Lord-for behold old things have passed away and now behold all things have become new, for you as you *sincerely repent* then I will restore what the canker worm has eaten up in you and remember your sins no more.

For there is only one sin I will not forgive and that is the sin of blasphemy-lack of reverence toward the Holy Spirit who is God which is the thinking of *yourself equal to God*...this is the unforgivable lie sin Satan committed and continues to lie and commit. Beloved we are not little Gods' and we will never be little Gods' as some preach.

It is very simple we will choose one way or another, the *pride of life-kingdoms of this world* the *way of Cane*, or the way of *Abel humility* and the *kingdom of God.*

Beloved through all the trials, tribulations and testing of our faith his love prepares us to "overcome by the blood of the lamb" that gives us our testimonies of his *great grace,* which is his love in our lives. Brace yourself hold fast to the Cross Church but beware if you defile the cross by habitually sinning and justifying it, for you 'will be left behind!

E. C.

I pray heavenly Father that I have grown up in Christ Jesus and am no longer justifying sin in my life for I know now what sin is and I am 'held accountable for this knowledge.

I can hear you all now, for I use to say the same thing making excuses for my bad behavior (sin) before the Word of God changed me now my desire is to please him and not my flesh. I thank God now for when I say or do something I should not I am repulsed by the sin, still in me and I repent and ask forgiveness from the Lord and when given the chance ask forgiveness from whoever I have offended. Because I stand in his present every day and it grieves me greatly to know I have sinned against him.

You say I go to church every Sunday confess, and repent for my sins, serve in the church, give to the poor and you are a good person you hurt no one. While you plan your week of sin filled destructive behavior like gathering for lunch, immoral movie, meetings of gossip, slandering, backbiting cheating your brother or sister, or planning to gamble, dance, party, joke about getting drunk, sleep with the man or women next door, or where ever you can find them! You call good evil and evil good and the best excuse ever is I am not perfect! Boy, are you right! Marriage no longer exists it is obsolete and old fashion yet the gays want it, that should tell you something! Do you think you take God's blessings for granted and you say *NO* in all this, you still call yourself a Christian?

Oh, how your flesh loves the prosperity, feel good look at me smile the entire time you have to feel good about yourself gospel on TV! Contrary to what the word of God, which states that God chastise those he loves least they are a bastard, and heaven forbid we might learn to obey through the things we suffer and to suffer for the gospel sake is obsolete! For the feel-good gospel feels so good and looks so good it tickles my ears like gossip, how can what feels so good be so bad! I call this the Adam and Eve *syndrome*

Syndrome a group of signs and symptoms that occur together and characterize a particular abnormality or condition

I believe gambling is so very destructive because it teaches you to *covet* and it seems so harmless and fun! Do you know gamblers to *covet* is the original sin Adam and Eve committed, they wanted to eat from the *tree of good and evil* and become just like God...and Lucifer made it sound so pleasurable to them and he made them over to be just like him it was so harmless I'm not hurting anyone. *Covet to desire enviously (what belongs to another)* God said no!

You hurt no one but your children and grandchildren for they learn by example! You want your children to like you so it is ok darlings as long as you do it at home for I can't bear to think of you out on the street alone having sex, drugs whatever do it at home! Then you place the biggest cross you can find somewhere and of course you go to church and pray for your wayward children or light a big candle. While at your home, you defame the cross before your children and the entire world. This is the biggest self-righteous lie of the Enemy for he knows we learn to obey through the things we suffer. For God chastises those he loves. There is nothing wrong with displaying the cross, but check your motives for God knows your heart. Lives, minds, homes name it the world is broken because of coveting after the things that God said no to.

There is great blessings in knowing who Jesus is let no man steal your crown. The tree of life bears twelve fruit for the healing of the nations...and Jesus chose twelve disciples.

My small thought on this scripture is, twelve is the number of Devine Government; apostolic fullness 'all will be revealed in his time for we are not to add or take away from this book. Rev. 22:1-21-read all of Revelations and be blessed.

The text in this book 'was derived from studying, reading hearing the Holy Bible from Gen. to Rev. K. J. V.

"Praise Him, Praise His Holy Name"

All honor, glory are yours Father, Son, Holy Spirit glory, glory, glory halleluiah to your "Most Holy Name" that is above every name and soon every knee shall bow and every tongue confess that Jesus Christ is Lord! Hell had me, till Jesus Christ delivered me' yes, yes, yes! Now I am a part of his beloved church and hell shall not prevail against it. Rejoice, rejoice, and rejoice again dance and sing before him' for his Davidic anointed children are hear coming to praise and worship him! From the four corners of the earth they are hear and more are coming for yes children shall lead us into the Holiness unto the Lord revival praising His Holy Name for soon' so very soon' every knee shall bow and every tongue confess that Jesus Christ is Lord!

If you doubt me, look on You-tube for the Lord led me to you-tube for confirmation the children are coming from everywhere praising him with beautiful voices...and some are yet to know who they are in him the humble ones the precious ones we do not deserve! I warn you do not even try to use them, to profit your greed. They are chosen vessels for we have hurt the little ones enough with our self-righteous, behavior.

Note: I have added some scripture text throughout this book but you must check it all out for yourself—*please study asking the Holy Spirit to help you.*

"Blessings" May the manifold

Blessings of the Lord over take you and shield you from false doctrine. I Cor. 14: 36—40 KJV